BASIC ECONOMIC
PROBLEMS

BASIC ECONOMIC PROBLEMS

A Christian Approach

by

JOHN F. SLEEMAN

Lecturer in Social Economics,
University of Glasgow

SCM PRESS LTD
56 BLOOMSBURY STREET
LONDON

First published 1953

Printed in Great Britain by
Northumberland Press Limited
Gateshead-on-Tyne

CONTENTS

CONTENTS

PREFACE

I hope that this book will be some help to those who want to arrive at a fuller understanding of the nature of the economic order. Such a fuller understanding is essential if our economic actions are to be responsible, and the need for responsible action cannot be evaded. After all, we are bound up with the economic order whether we like it or not. When we do our daily work to get our living, or when we draw our dividends on our invested capital, we are inevitably taking part in the process of production. When we buy our necessary food and clothing, pay rent for our houses, or spend money on pleasures and luxuries, we have an equally inevitable influence as consumers. When we save money and put it in the bank, or buy shares with it, we are influencing the level of saving and investment, and so on. We affect the working of the system by the way we do our work and spend our incomes, and we are affected in turn by what others do.

Economic action is thus unavoidable, but responsible action is difficult, for several reasons. In the first place, the social and economic order is so vast and complex, and our own direct part in it is so small, that we are apt to feel that the whole thing is too big for us. We do not know enough about the problems involved, so we cannot do anything very useful. In the second place, we have come to see how much we are bound up with society ourselves, and how much our habitual ways of thinking and standards of judgment are influenced by the accepted beliefs of the social order in which we live. We feel that it is too difficult to get outside it, so to speak, and to make really objective criticisms of it.

Because our thoughts and actions are so much influenced by

society, goodwill alone is not enough. It is not enough to be decent and kindly and to want to help others and treat them fairly. This is very important, but it does not go deep enough. Nor can we be content with upholding right standards of conduct only in our direct personal relationships, with our own family and friends and those with whom we come into face to face contact. We have got to tackle the social order also, to try to understand how it works and what it is for and what it is intended to be like.

It is here that our sub-title 'A Christian Approach' comes in. After all, Christianity is supposed to be able to give us an objective standard of judgment and to have something to say, not only about personal relations, but about the whole of society.

The book is written from an avowedly Christian standpoint. It starts from the Christian beliefs concerning the nature of God and man. Its theme is that Christianity is in fact concerned with the whole of life, including the economic order as an essential part of it. If this is true, it means Christianity has a gospel for the economic order, if only we can come to understand it. It also means that it demands a response from us in the whole of life, in our economic activities as much as in any others. In this conviction the attempt is made to bring together the economist's specialized understanding of the way in which the system actually works, and the theological understanding of the nature of the universe derived from the Faith.

At the same time, it is hoped that it will be of value to all men and women of goodwill who are concerned with these problems, whether they would accept the Christian explanation of the world or not. It does not claim to provide any solutions, but it does claim to suggest lines of thought which may prove fruitful. I would venture to commend it therefore to the industrialist or business man, the trade union leader, the teacher, the social worker and the parson, to mention only a few of those whose work compels them to think about these matters. And to my fellow academic economists also I hope it may not be without interest, for it represents an attempt to break down the barriers which so often tend to cut off our professional thinking from our responsibilities as citizens and our attempts to arrive at a satisfactory philosophy of life. Indeed, if it does something to counteract the modern curse of the excessive compartmentalization of knowledge, it will be well worth while for that alone.

I am greatly indebted to the following for their encouraging interest and their valuable suggestions, which have helped to make the book possible: Professor A. L. Macfie and Mr. D. J. Robertson, of Glasgow University; Professor Duncan Black, now of the University College of North Wales, Bangor; Mr. D. L. Munby, of Aberdeen University; Rev. R. H. Preston, of Manchester University; and Rev. J. D. McCaughey, formerly of the S.C.M. Press.

J.F.S.

February, 1953.

CHAPTER ONE

INTRODUCTION—THE NEED FOR AN ECONOMIC PHILOSOPHY

1. Economics and Economic Philosophy.

Christian men and women need guidance in the exercise of their economic responsibility. In this generation we are coming to a new realization of the significance of our assertion that Christ is the Lord of all life. He is the Lord not only of our personal relationships with Him and with our neighbours, but of the corporate activities of men also. He is the Lord of politics and economics and of the whole organization of society, and, in so far as men do not recognize His Rule, they cannot expect society to function harmoniously, nor can they expect their deepest needs to be satisfied. Therefore we are called as Christians to serve God not only in our personal relationships, but in the way in which we do our work and get our living. In order that we may try to do this more effectively, two things are necessary.

First, there must be an understanding of the nature of the field in which this responsibility is to be exercised. That is, of the way in which the economic system works: the way in which mankind gets its living. This is the province of that system of scientific analysis to which we give the name of economics. The study of economics, like the study of any other branch, either of the natural order or of human activity, is, within its own limitations, a scientific discipline with its own independent validity. Just as one must go to physics or chemistry or astronomy if one wants to find out how the inanimate universe

11

functions, or to biology if one wants to discover the workings of living organisms, so one must go to economics if one wants to find out how in fact the economic system works.

It is true that economics, as a social science, concerned with one aspect of the working of human society, is in some respects different from the natural sciences. For one thing, it cannot use the method of controlled experiment to test its hypotheses. For another thing, since it is concerned with the interactions of the motives and decision of a large number of human beings, its data are apt to be more complex and less uniform than those of the natural sciences, and its laws to have a lesser degree of precision and certainty. The 'other things' which have to be assumed to remain equal when stating an economic law are so varied that they are in fact unlikely to remain equal. Moreover, since economics is concerned with human actions, it cannot avoid consideration of human motives and ideals, since these are part of the data. Assumptions have to be made about human conduct under certain circumstances, and these assumptions are bound to be unduly narrow and to that extent unrealistic. Yet, in spite of all these limitations, economic theory, in so far as it is tested by its correspondence to observed facts, remains a valid explanation of that aspect of human life which is its proper sphere. It remains true that if we are to understand how the economic system works, and the significance of economic problems and choices, it is to economics that we must go for guidance.

In the second place, having gained as full an understanding as is possible of the facts of how mankind gets its living, it is necessary to try to see the economic system in which we are involved in the light of what as Christians we believe to be God's purposes for mankind and the universe. Here we pass from the field of economics in the scientific sense into that of what we may call economic philosophy. By this we mean the attempt to interpret the facts of the economic system in the light of what we believe to be the fundamental values of the universe—in terms of our 'world-view', if you like. We pass from the question: 'How does the system work?' to the question: 'Why does it work?' 'What purposes does it fulfil and what purposes ought it to fulfil, and how can it be made to fulfil them more successfully?'

2. *The need for a Christian economic philosophy.*

Economic philosophies will naturally vary according to the fundamental beliefs of those who formulate them. A Christian economic philosophy will not be the same as a Marxist one, nor as that of a liberal humanist. Nor will all Christians necessarily arrive at the same philosophy. Every thinker on economic matters will tend, even if only implicitly, to work out his own economic philosophy, in terms of his own basic beliefs, which again may be implicit or explicit. It is because this is so that the need arises which the present book is trying to solve. While there have been many economists who have been Christians, it is unfortunately true that the main body of economic thought has tended to grow up without reference to Christian doctrine, and also that Christian social thinking has tended to take place without reference to economic doctrine. Ever since the breakdown to the medieval synthesis, it is true on the whole to say that there has not been a Christian economic philosophy. This is one symptom of that departmentalization of thought which has been the accompaniment of the vast expansion of knowledge in recent centuries. There has been a tendency to think in terms of 'economics' as one branch of study, to be pursued independently by experts, and 'theology' as another. This is an undoubted practical necessity, but it has its dangers. It remains true that while economics is concerned with one aspect of man's life, and theology with another, yet it is the same man who is involved in both, and his life and personality cannot be split up to correspond to the frontiers of the different disciplines. Moreover, to the Christian the theological aspect is the primary one, the one from which all the others draw their significance and in the light of which they must all be judged.

In this book, therefore, we are concerned to attempt to trace the main lines of a Christian economic philosophy, and also to examine some of its implications for Christians involved in the practical problems of everyday life. In the next three chapters, we shall try to discover what is the significance of the economic order in God's purposes and therefore what is the general nature of the Christian responsibility in the economic field. Later, we shall consider the economic system under which we live, and try to assess its achievements and shortcomings in the light of God's purposes as we have seen them. We shall also discuss some of the issues which arise, and the choices which have to be made, in certain particular fields of economic activity. Among them are: the distribution of incomes, full employment, Budget policy and Government expenditure, free enterprise and monopolies, and nationalization.

Turning first, therefore, to the economic order in God's purposes, we take our starting point, where Christians must take it, from the Sovereignty of God.

CHAPTER TWO

THE STARTING POINT

1. We must start from the Source and the Sovereign of all life.

All Christian thinking about the nature of the universe and
the purposes of human activity must start from God. God is the
Creator and Sustainer of all life. He has made all things and
He intends them to be used to His glory. He has redeemed all
things in Christ and made it possible by His grace for them to be
restored to the perfection which is His intention for them.
He sustains and inspires and directs all things by His Holy
Spirit.

God is therefore the King of all life. He reigns over all life
and it is His purpose to sum up all things in Christ. Those who
have experienced His redemptive love in Christ are called upon
to make their loving response by proclaiming Christ as the Lord
of all life—in the words of the motto of the Industrial Christian
Fellowship. He is to be served and glorified and His Will
is to be done in the economic order, as in all other branches of
human activity. Only when men seek to do His Will can the
economic order be expected to function effectively, for only then
is it being worked in the way in which its Creator and King
intends.

*2. The economic order as an essential sphere of God's creative
and redemptive activity.*

Since the economic order, the means by which we get our living, is an essential part of human life, it is an essential sphere of
God's creative and redemptive purpose. God has ordained the

economic order just as much as He has ordained any other part of human activity, and He intends it to be used to His glory. He is to be glorified and praised in the way in which men co-operate in using His gifts to satisfy their needs. The economic order, like the rest of creation, partakes in the Fall. Like all men's activities, it is vitiated by sin, whence come self-seeking, injustice and exploitation. Like the rest of creation, as we have seen, it partakes also in God's great act of redemption in Christ. Christ's redemption is to be made manifest in the way in which we get our living just as much as in other fields, such as personal relations or politics. Therefore the call to share in the resurrection power and to live out the redeemed life comes to us in our daily work and in our economic relationships, since these are an inescapable part of our life as a whole.

3. The call to discipleship in the economic order is inescapable.

The call to Christian discipleship in the economic order is inescapable because the economic order is inescapable. We cannot contract out of it if we would, for we are dependent on the co-operation of our fellows in order to get our living. Nor is it God's intention that we should evade responsibility for it, since it is one of the essential aspects of life. It is not an unfortunate necessity, to be accepted grudgingly with as little taking of responsibility as possible, as a hindrance to 'higher' and more 'spiritual' concerns. Such an attitude is impossible to the followers of the Son of Man who earned his living in a carpenter's shop. On the contrary, as we shall see more fully in the following chapter, it is a field in which positive discipleship is called for, in which there can be fellowship and co-operation, the sharing of gifts and the development of talents, and the use of God's good gifts to His glory.

Moreover, the attempt to evade the call and limit our responsibility brings dangers. It brings dangers to our own individual Christian life, which tends to become self-centred and unreal and pervaded by a false other-worldliness if we do not think out and accept responsibilities in so important a sector of our daily lives. It brings dangers from the point of view of the Church also. Where Christian witness in the social and economic order is neglected, the result is that Christian standards and values come to be confined to purely personal relationships, and the values of the world come to be accepted by default in wider social and economic relationships. Christianity comes to be thought of as a mere system of pietism, concerned only with escape from the world, and with nothing to say about the problems of daily life which affect men's lives at every turn, whether they realize it or not.

The fact that in recent centuries Christianity has often been felt to have nothing to say about economic relationships, except in terms of what were felt to be pious platitudes, is one reason for the lessening of its hold on the imaginations of men which accompanied the development of modern industrialism. Particularly has this been so in the case of the great mass of the industrial workers, who feel the conditions of their daily lives and the background of their personal relationships to be continually influenced and profoundly affected by economic factors. Because we have failed to think out the significance of our modern industrial society, and of its values and problems, in the light of God's purposes for the world, as we see them in our Faith, we have not been able to show the relevance of that Faith to those who feel their lives to be largely conditioned by such forces.

In saying this we are not, of course, undervaluing the primary importance of the personal experience of God in Christ, nor of the need for individual salvation. What we are emphasizing is that the individual is not an isolated unit, but a member of a community, intended to love his neighbour and live in fellowship with him. Salvation therefore cannot be a matter only of the direct relationship between the individual and God: it must extend to all his relationships with his fellows, of which the economic relationships are among the most important.

17   B

Concern for economic and social righteousness can never be a substitute for individual salvation, but it is both an expression of it and a means to it.

We have thus seen that the economic order has an essential part in God's creative and redemptive purposes. In the next chapter we shall try to examine in more detail what that part is.

CHAPTER THREE

THE PURPOSE OF THE ECONOMIC ORDER

1. *The right use of good gifts—co-operation in creation and enjoyment.*

The starting point of our argument in the last chapter was that we live in a world of which God is Creator and King. It is with the use which He intends men to make of His creation that we shall be concerned in this chapter. For an appropriate theme we can take the words attributed to God in the story of the Creation, as related in the first chapter of Genesis. 'And God saw everything which he had made and behold, it was very good.' This is an essential affirmation in any Christian doctrine of the economic order. God's world is good. He has given His good gifts to be used by men to His glory. They are His gifts and He intends men to enjoy them.

The gifts of God to men are in a two-fold form. There are the natural resources of the world, of land and sea and sky, mineral and vegetable and animal. There are also the skills and powers of man's brain and hand by which to develop and use them. Man is given God's good gifts freely, but he is called upon to co-operate with God in making them available more fully and richly to his own enjoyment and God's glory. It is by work that man is called upon to earn his living, and work is intended to be a co-operation with God in His creative work.

It is true that this world, in which man is thus called to free and joyful co-operation with God in the development and enjoyment of the riches of creation, is marred by sin. It is

19

because of the fallen nature of mankind and of the universe that man sets himself against the purposes to which he is called by his Creator and seeks what he considers to be his own self-interest, so that what should be joyful co-operation is felt to be arduous drudgery. This is the more so since it is often performed under conditions of injustice and exploitation. But Christianity teaches us that the economic order shares in God's redemptive work in Christ, and that by His grace it can once again become what it is intended to be.

2. *Economic activity as a means of fellowship and co-operation between men.*

The activity of getting our living is one in which we are dependent on our fellows. This is true even of the most primitive communities, in which some degree of division of labour and mutual dependence is practised. It has become increasingly true as the economic order has become more complex, until in our modern industrial world we are required to co-operate in getting our living with millions of our fellows throughout the world, and are dependent on them in turn for all the necessities and enjoyments of life.

Man has been created as a social being, one who can only develop the fullness of his individual personality in fellowship with his neighbours. This is easily realized in the sphere of direct personal relationships, but it is just as true in the economic sphere. Economic activity, which plays such a large part in our waking lives, is intended to be a means of fellowship and co-operation, not only between man and God, but also between man and his neighbour. It is a sphere in which we are called upon to love our neighbours as ourselves.

This is an important principle to bear in mind when later we come to criticize the actual working of economic institutions. The making of the best and fullest use of the world's resources by the skill of man to God's glory depends upon harmonious co-operation. Each must give of his best and must show consideration for the well-being of others rather than being over-eager to take of the best for himself. Such harmony and co-operation depend essentially on self-giving for a common cause rather than on self-seeking. Yet in man's nature as we know it self-seeking is a strong and persistent element, and one that tends to dominate social organizations unless it is subdued by a stronger loyalty.

3. *The economic principle—the economizing of scarce resources —in its truest sense is an application of the principle of stewardship.*

Men are therefore called upon, in fellowship with God and with one another, to make the best use of the available resources of raw materials and labour and of their accumulated products in the form of capital. At any given time or place, the supplies of their productive resources which are in fact available are limited relative to the uses to which they could be put. Man's potential wants, on the other hand, which could be met if the resources could be provided, are infinite and capable of constant development with experience. There is therefore a problem of choice. We have to choose which wants are to be satisfied, since they cannot all be, and also in what ways the available productive resources are to be used in order to make it possible to satisfy them.

It is in this question of choice between alternative uses of scarce resources to satisfy needs that the central economic problem arises. If the most effective use is to be made of the available resources, we have to economize them, as we say. They must be divided between alternative uses and we have to decide what is the most effective way in which to combine them.

We must therefore establish some criterion of the most effective use. Normally, in what is known as 'welfare economics', this is taken to be that which produces a greater degree of satisfaction of wants than any alternative combination. The difficulty, of course, is to measure and compare the extent of satisfaction, since this is an individual and personal matter not capable of addition and comparison as between persons. For the Christian, the criterion ideally should be that use of resources which provides for the greatest enjoyment of God's gifts to His glory and which hence is most in accordance with His Will. But God has laid on us the responsibility of using our own intelligence and insight into His purposes to work out what this means in terms of practical situations. We have to decide what goods and services are in fact to be produced and how they are to be distributed.

However difficult the application of a criterion to particular cases may be, the principle itself of making the most economical use of resources, or principle of economy as we may call it for short, is both sound and important. In its truest sense, and in the obligation which it lays upon us in the making of our own economic choices, it is an application of that principle of stewardship which has always been accepted Christian doctrine concerning the use both of material wealth and of personal talents. We are, however, called to accept responsibility for the exercise of stewardship, not only in our individual choices concerning the use we make of our incomes or our talents, but also in the choices which society as a whole makes in the use of its productive resources for the satisfying of human needs. It is thus the responsibility of stewardship which impels us to concern ourselves with the part which the economic order plays in God's purposes, how far it is playing that part in the world as we know it, and in what directions this economic order might be modified in order to bring it nearer to these purposes.

Resources must be divided in the most economical way, not only as between varying uses for the satisfying of different kinds of wants at the present time, but also as between their use by present and future generations. The doctrine of stewardship and the principle of economy are concerned, for instance, when it is a case of the reckless using up of mineral resources, or the cutting down of forests without replanting, or of the over-cropping of land at the expense of its fertility, or of the despoilment of land of agricultural value or natural beauty for the sake of an increase of industrial prosperity which may be only temporary. In all such cases there is a responsibility for wise and far-seeing choices.

4. *We cannot evade the challenge of increasing economic wealth so long as so many lack necessities and ordinary comforts.*

If God's world is good and His gifts are intended to be enjoyed by His children to His glory, it follows that an increase of economic wealth is in itself good. This is true although man in his selfishness misuses the gifts, using his skill and the world's natural resources to produce forms of wealth which may be harmful instead of good, or at any rate making use of the products which are themselves useful in ways which are harmful. Yet although wealth can be, and is, misused, an increasing flow of goods and services, an increasing availability of the necessities and ordinary comforts of life cannot but be regarded as good. We cannot but believe that God intends all His children to have enough to eat, decent homes and adequate clothing, and the opportunity to share in those amenities of fuller and more worth-while living to which we give the name of civilization. And this is true, although it is true also that these things will be perverted and become a source of curse instead of blessing unless they are received as gifts from God and used to His glory. The Christian teaching about wealth is concerned with the right use and thankful acceptance of gifts which are good, not with the dangers of something which is itself evil. To say this is not to minimize the dangers of the misuse of wealth. Because men are selfish, the likelihood is that the process of increasing wealth will be accompanied by self-seeking exploitation on the part of the individuals, or classes, or nations, which are in a more favourable position and by neglect of the interests of those less favourably situated.

We can say this the more confidently when we recall that in all ages up to the present, and for most of the world's inhabitants in the present age, an adequate supply of the necessities and comforts of life has been denied to all but a minority. It is only in very recent years that such an adequate minimum standard has become available to the peoples of western Europe and North America, and this is largely the result of their privileged position, in relation to the rest of the world, as the main centres of the development of mechanized industry. If we are tempted to complacency, we have only to remember the conditions of the majority of the people of India, China, Africa, the Middle East or South America, or even in eastern Europe. We in Britain have been unpleasantly reminded in recent years of the relatively precarious nature of our position, dependent as we are on the export of manufactured goods and of services to the rest of the world in order to pay for the import of most of our foodstuffs and raw materials.

In face of such a situation, there is a constant challenge to the human race to rise to the destiny to which their Creator has called them. It is a challenge to make, by His guidance, a more truly economical use of the available natural resources, human skill and experience and accumulated capital. The vision of 'poverty in the midst of plenty', implying that the problem of production had been solved and the sole problem was that of distribution, which haunted the imagination of the West in the 1930's, has been proved, by the destruction and dislocation of war and its aftermath and by the experience of full employment, to be an illusion. The world's problem is still one of poverty, of production inadequate to meet the need. The problem is accentuated by the rapid increase of population in many parts of the world, as a result of the weakening through scientific development and improved security of the Malthusian checks of disease and disorder, without any consequent limita-

tion of families such as has come to redress the balance in the
west. In view of this situation, an increase of material wealth,
an increase in the available flow of goods and services to meet
men's needs, can be seen to be an urgent necessity, unless hunger
and poverty and disease are to retain their sway over the greater
part of the world. The greatest need of course is for increased
food production, but this will only be possible if there is an
increase of industrial production also, both to supply the capital
goods necessary to increased agricultural production, and to
reduce the pressure of population of the land, for increased
agricultural productivity involves a smaller proportion of the
population engaged in agriculture and a larger proportion
engaged in industry and services. The mainly industrial
countries thus have a part to play which is just as essential
as that of the more agricultural countries.

5. Involuntary poverty is not God's Will.

This question of the Christian doctrine of wealth, and of the
place in God's purposes of the economic aim of increasing
material wealth, needs further discussion. At first sight there
may appear to be a conflict between what has been said above,
and the emphasis in Christian thought, and especially in our
Lord's own teaching, on the serious dangers of riches. How
can we say that it is in accordance with God's Will that we
should seek to maximize the available flow of goods and services,
and at the same time assert that it is easier for a camel to go
through the eye of a needle than for a rich man to enter into
the Kingdom of Heaven? The paradox is unavoidable in a
sinful world. Nevertheless, what is denounced by our Lord as
dangerous is not riches themselves so much as the trust in
them. He is concerned to point out the undoubted dangers to
the soul of man, and the undoubted injustice to his fellows,
that arise from the pursuit of riches as one of the dominant
aims of life, or equally from the care to maintain and

increase and enjoy as one's own the fruits of riches already possessed.

Our Lord, who cared so much for men's bodily well-being that He was always ready to heal the sick and to share in the enjoyment of good fellowship, and even to provide food for His followers, certainly did not put forward any idea of material things being evil in themselves. Rather, He regarded them as the good gifts of His Heavenly Father, and told His disciples to trust in Him, because their Father knew their need of them.

Voluntary poverty, the deliberate renunciation of the riches of the world, has played a large part in Christian tradition. It was practised by Christ Himself and by His first followers and has been practised by many Christians since, for a definite purpose, to free themselves from entanglements that would hamper their loyalty to God and their service of Him. But acquiescence in the endurance of involuntary poverty by others is another matter. Because Christ calls His followers not to be too much attached to what the world regards as the worth-while things, that does not mean that He does not intend them to be concerned that their fellows should have enough of this world's goods to enable them to develop their capacities as God intends. Poverty forced on men by circumstances is usually an ugly and cramping thing, which hampers such fuller development and tends to warp character. True, if accepted it can become a means of grace, as can any other form of suffering, but just as we cannot believe that sickness is God's purpose for anyone, so we cannot believe that He intends His children to endure poverty.

We may therefore hold that it is in accordance with God's Will that economic wealth should be increased so that there shall be enough for all to enjoy. This is only the first stage in the argument, however. We have still to consider how the production of goods and services is organized. We have to consider not only whether it is organized to make possible this primary purpose, but also what the effects of the forms of organization are likely to be on human personality. Economic activity,

as we saw above, is intended to be one form of human fellowship, and we have to judge the type of relationships to which
it gives rise by this criterion. We have also to consider the
implications of how the available product is distributed, and
what use is made of the product by the recipients.

6. The self-regarding instinct is the main incentive to economic activity in an imperfect world.

The conflict between the increase of wealth to make possible
the fuller enjoyment of God's good gifts by His children, and
the dangers of the love of riches, arises, as we have seen, out
of man's fallen nature.

Man is created by God in His own image, capable of respond-
ing to His love, but he is also by nature prone to self-seeking—
to putting himself in the place of God. The self-regarding
instinct, in all its forms, including the desire to do the best
not only for oneself, but also for one's dependents, is one of
the strongest and most fundamental elements in human nature.
In itself it is of course essential to survival, and in this sense
it is properly to be regarded as God-given. But it is not intended
to become an end in itself, but to find its fulfilment in self-
surrender to the service of the Creator. Man, however, is not
content to use his self-regarding instinct as a means of self-
preservation to fit him for the better service of God. He sets
up self-will and self-seeking in opposition to the will of God
for him.

The self-regarding instinct has always been probably the main
incentive to economic activity. Economic activity was undertaken first of all in the interests of direct survival, to secure by
one's own efforts the necessary food, shelter and security for
oneself and one's family. As economic organization became
more complex, the impact of self-regard came to take a less
direct form. The aim became rather to secure command over
goods and services in the form of a money reward. From the

necessity to earn a living, self-interest easily impels towards the accumulation of greater riches to secure a greater command over goods and services, or to gain less tangible forms of reward such as the power and prestige of wealth and success, or the greater opportunities which it brings.

Because man is idealistic as well as self-seeking, the self-regarding motive is often sublimated into the seeking of the interest of the wider group of which the individual feels himself to be a member. Thus desire to do the best for one's family may often be a stronger, and more fruitful motive, than desire to benefit oneself. Similarly, the interest of a group of families, or clan, has often played a large part in inspiring economic activities. On a wider scale, loyalty to the interests of a social or economic class may be an important factor, and on a still wider scale, loyalty to the nation or country. Thus the distinction between self-interest and the interest of the neighbour is by no means clear-cut, for no man can be entirely self-sufficient. Yet none of these loyalties is enough by itself to transcend the force of self-interest, for loyalty to those in the group tends to be balanced by hostility to those outside it.

Self-regard has never been the only motive to economic activity. There have always been others, such as the satisfaction of creation, whether it be that of a craftsman making a chair or a vase, or helping to build a ship, or that of the professional man exercising his skill, or the artist, writer or musician, or that of the business man building up a great and successful industrial or commercial concern. There has also often been a genuine sense of serving the community, the satisfaction of knowing that one is doing a necessary job and doing it well. More consciously altruistic motives, including a true sense of vocation in the service of God, have not been lacking either. But the self-regarding motive, in the wide sense in which it includes obligation to family, is so strong that it has usually been relied upon to get the world's work done. This is the more true in that so much necessary work is of the drab and

monotonous sort, such that it is very difficult for anyone to
find any creative satisfaction in doing it.

7. *The self-regarding motive does not go far enough.*

That this driving force is strong and effective nobody will
deny. Human nature being what it is, it is probable that it
cannot be dispensed with in an unredeemed world. We have
seen in our own day a renewed emphasis on the importance of
'incentives' to more efficient production and harder work,
particularly under conditions of full employment and the planned
economy, when the incentives of profit and the fear of the sack
are weakened in their effect. But because it is self-regarding
it has its limitations. If economic activity is inspired mainly by
the seeking of advantage for self by those who take part in it,
it cannot in the long run produce harmony and co-operation.
There may be co-operation on the part of groups who feel themselves to have a common interest, but they will be in conflict
with other groups whose interests are opposed. The best that
can be achieved is a clash and interaction of opposing interests,
out of which by some self-regulating mechanism, or through
some 'invisible hand', the greatest attainable good for the
greatest number may be hoped to be somehow achieved. As
we shall see later, the acceptance of this position is the basis of
the theory of free enterprise and the competitive market. We
shall be concerned to assess the relative merits of reliance on
this system of automatic self-regulation through the interaction
of competing interests, as against attempts to plan and control
the working of the system by deliberate action.

Unfortunately the protagonists are not equal in ability or
opportunity. There are always those who are cleverer or luckier
or more persistent than their fellows. It is on their energy and
enterprise that the success of the system depends, it is true, but
if the pursuit of self-interest is unchecked, they soon gain an
advantage which becomes cumulative, since they in turn can

give a better start to their children. Thus the reliance on the self-regarding motive, while it provides the driving force for economic progress and the increase of wealth, also gives scope for injustice and exploitation, through the abuse by those who possess them of their superior abilities or opportunities. It is because of this element of self-seeking in men that the increase of wealth, in itself good, becomes an occasion of evil, and riches come to be a snare to the possessor and a cause of oppression and hardship to others.

The economic order can thus be seen to be in need of redemption. The self-regarding motive is not to be rejected as evil. It corresponds to something essential in man, being necessary for the will to survival, and for the expression of individuality. Man must be given freedom to develop his individual capabilities through the way in which he gets his living. Given the nature of man, it is an essential driving force, but it is not enough in itself. Man needs a loyalty to something outside himself if he is to transcend self and give of his full powers to the common good. Self-interest needs to be sublimated into a wider and fuller ideal, which will be capable of inspiring devotion and self-sacrifice. In no area of life is this need greater than in the economic, where self-interest has tended to hold the field more strongly than elsewhere. It is this becoming aware of a power and a purpose greater than oneself which calls forth the loyalty of the individual and enlists all his energy and intelligence and knowledge and skill, to an even greater extent than self-interest can do, that is of the essence of redemption, as the Church experiences it in Christ. It is for us in the Church to work out by our own thinking and action what are the implications of the redeemed life in terms of our economic witness, and in what forms the message of redemption is to be shown forth to the world around us in economic terms. To that purpose this book is intended to be a contribution.

CHAPTER FOUR

THE CRITERIA
OF AN ECONOMIC ORDER WHICH
FULFILS GOD'S PURPOSE

1. *No actual human society can achieve such aims, because of sin. They represent rather a sketching of the standards and ideals by which to judge actual economic orders.*

In the light of what we have considered in the previous chapter concerning the part which the economic order plays in God's purpose, we can go on to consider what would be the characteristics of an economic order which fulfilled these purposes. Here a note of caution must first be sounded. Because of human sin, and the limitations of man's knowledge and understanding, all forms of human society are bound to be inadequate and imperfect, both in their aims and still more in their realization of them. Therefore when we consider the characteristics of an economic order which fulfilled God's purposes, we must not be taken to be describing any actual society, either past or present or in prospect. We are rather trying to work out standards of judgment by which we can criticize the actual aims and achievements of existing societies, in the hope of suggesting the lines along which Christian witness could fruitfully be made. The practical aim is to help in the more effective doing of God's Will by His servants in the situation in which they find themselves.

Similarly, when we try to assess the merits and the shortcomings of the economic order as we have known it, and discuss possible alternatives, the same considerations must be borne in mind. The aim cannot be merely to condemn an existing form of order as 'un-Christian' and to advocate an alternative form as 'Christian', nor can it be the reverse. The outward forms of economic organization, like those of society as a whole, tend to reflect the changing techniques and needs and ways of thought of successive ages. Therefore we must expect the forms of the economic order, as of the political and the social, to be constantly changing and developing. We cannot say conclusively on *a priori* grounds that large-scale private enterprise capitalism is more, or less, 'Christian' than small-scale domestic craftsmanship, or that a predominantly industrial economy is more, or less, 'Christian' in itself than a predominantly agricultural one. Nor can we say that the public ownership of the means of production is in itself more, or less, 'Christian' than private ownership, though we can draw attention to the typical characteristics and consequences of each. Each represents a particular form of organization, adapted to certain conditions of social and technical and administrative development. Each must be expected to contain a mixture of good and evil, both in its aims and in its achievements.

Yet, behind the changing forms of organization, the essential purposes of the economic order still remain. As Christians we believe that God has a purpose for His creation and that the economic order has an essential part to play in it. This purpose can be fulfilled, or otherwise, by means of an infinite variety of forms of organization. Essentially it is a matter of the spirit and the motives which underlie and inspire economic activity and of the ends which it is designed to secure rather than of the details of the outward forms. At the same time, the outward forms are both an expression of, and themselves have an effect on, the aims and motives. There is therefore a Christian duty of carrying out, through the insight given by the Holy Spirit, a sort of continuous critique on the working of the economic system, both in its motives and ideas, and in its outward forms. This must, however, be done humbly and carefully, with a full realization of the limitation of our own vision, and the extent to which we ourselves are affected by the spirit of the age, both in what we accept and in what we condemn.

2. *Some of the criteria by which the economic order can be judged.*

With these provisos in mind, we can now proceed to draw up some of the standards of judgment which we can apply to the working of existing forms of economic organization and to possible modifications of them. We shall consider them first under the two main heads of economic efficiency and human efficiency.

A. Economic efficiency—i.e. making the most effective provision for the satisfaction of men's wants to God's glory.

The first and most essential criterion of any economic order is how effectively it fulfils its primary function of economizing productive resources. How effective is it in making the best use of scarce means of production, both natural and human and accumulated, for the satisfaction of men's wants in such a way that they may to the fullest extent enjoy God's gifts to His glory?

Under the general heading of economic efficiency, as we may call it, there are a number of sub-headings which we can distinguish, which correspond to the chief essential functions which any economic order must perform. It is by their effectiveness for the carrying out of these functions that the economic efficiency of particular forms of organization can best be judged.

(i) *The Problem of Demand—which wants are to be satisfied?*

The first function is that of tackling the problem of demand. By this we mean the way in which it is decided which of the illimitable human wants shall in fact be satisfied. In other words, how is it decided what types of goods and services shall in fact

C

be produced for consumption and in what quantities and qualities respectively? How do we decide between more food or more television sets, more guns or more butter, more houses or more factories, or between more, cheaper, poorer quality clothes and fewer, dearer, better quality clothes, and so on?

> (ii) *The Problem of Production—How are productive resources to be combined in order to satisfy these wants?*

Secondly comes the problem of production. This is the problem of deciding how the various productive resources, or factors of production as we call them, are to be combined so as to produce the goods and services demanded in the most economical way. How is it decided what use is to be made of the different types of raw material, the different human skills, the different types of capital such as buildings and machines? Obviously the demand problem and the production, or supply, problem, interact continuously and closely. Ultimately, demand is primary, since production is undertaken to supply human wants, but at any given time, supply conditions in turn greatly affect demand. The relative terms on which different kinds of goods and services can be made available obviously affect the relative demand for them. If a certain product can be made available more cheaply, the demand for it will generally increase, whereas if another is scarce and costly to produce, the demand for it will tend to decrease, and these changes will affect the demand for other goods. In the short period, therefore, the decision which wants are to be supplied is often as much that of the producer as of the consumer.

> (iii) *The Problem of Exchange—On what terms are the various goods and services exchanged among those who produce them and consume them?*

The next problem is that of Exchange. How, and on what

terms, are the various goods and services exchanged among those who took part in producing them and those who want to consume them? What determines the relative terms on which different types of goods and services are exchanged against each other? In terms of a market economy, such as we are familiar with, this is a question of relative price levels and the interaction of supply and demand in the market.

> (iv) *The Problem of Distribution—How is the command over goods and services divided among the owners of the factors of production?*

The problem of Distribution is the obverse of that of Exchange. In considering it we are concerned, not with the relative exchange values of goods and services, but with the division of the command over goods and services between those who are the controllers of the factors of production, such as labour, land and capital, which take part in the productive process, and also between those who for various reasons do not contribute to it. For the most part, in the economy as we know it, this is a question of the distribution of money incomes between different classes of income-receivers. Even in our own economy, however, it can take other forms, such as the payment of income in kind, the right to perquisites, rationing, the consumption of home-made goods.

> (v) *The Problem of Saving and Investment— How is the product divided between present consumption and the maintenance and improvement of productive capacity?*

Finally there is the problem of how the product of the economy is divided between present consumption of goods and services, and the setting aside of resources to maintain the present productive capacity intact, or to extend and improve it. A certain proportion of the product must be saved by being withdrawn from consumption and must be invested, either in depreciation and maintenance of existing capital, or in the provision of new capital to make possible a larger and more economically produced product in the future.

These five functions must be performed, in some form or other, by any economic system. It is therefore useful, when assessing the economic efficiency of any particular form of organization, to examine it with reference to the way in which it performs them, and the results which are produced. We shall use them as criteria when we come on to criticize our own economic system. Meanwhile we must pass on from economic efficiency to the second main head of human efficiency.

B. Human Efficiency—i.e. making possible the fullest development of the personalities and capacities of those who take part in economic activity, to God's glory.

The criterion of what we may call human efficiency comes second only to the primary criterion of economic efficiency. How far do the outward forms and the inner motives of economic activity encourage the fullest development of the personalities and capabilities of the men and women who are inescapably involved in them? How far does the way in which they get their living help or hinder them in becoming the sort of people God intends them to be? An economic order which made possible the fullest and most economical provision of goods and services for the satisfaction of men's wants, and the fairest distribution of them, would still be open to condemnation if in the process of gaining these goods and services for their enjoyment, men's natures were warped and perverted by the conditions under which they earned and spent their livings.

There are three related aspects of this problem of human efficiency. They are the provision of creative opportunity, the provision of fellowship and the inspiration of a common purpose.

36

(i) *Satisfaction of man's need for creative opportunity.*

In the first place, as we have seen, God has called men to co-operate with Him in His creative work. He has made us so that we only develop to the fullest extent of our capacities if we have the opportunity of using our powers in some form of creative activity. These creative powers are given to men in very different forms and in very different degrees, but they are given to all men. It must surely be God's purpose that our daily work, which occupies such a large part of our waking lives, should provide scope for their exercise. There is an immediate challenge to us here, in that so much of the necessary work of the world is essentially dull and uninteresting and provides little creative scope. This is one sphere in which the need for redemption is obvious. Perhaps we get a hint as to the way if we think of our Lord working in the carpenter's shop, where, along with creative work of the craftsman, there must have been much routine drudgery also. All work, however dull and arduous, can be done to God's glory, if it can be seen as part of His purpose. But this is not the whole answer. We still have the responsibility of seeing that we use the abilities which God has given us as far as possible to reduce the extent of drudgery and to make it possible for all to have the work that is best suited to their talents. In this respect there are both credit and debit items in the record of modern industrialism. The use of machinery has undoubtedly done away with much hard manual drudgery and has increased the variety of opportunities of different kinds of work available. At the same time it has introduced problems of its own, especially through the development of mass-production and assembly-line methods.

(ii) *Satisfaction of man's need for fellowship and co-operation.*

Secondly, as we have seen also, God intends men to live in

fellowship with one another, and their work and other economic activities are intended to be a field in which this fellowship can find expression through co-operation in a common task. Men must be able to find in their work a sense of common effort and mutual give and take in the achievement of a common aim. Through the relationships involved in work, they should come to know and value one another as persons mutually necessary to one another. One of the redeeming features of modern industrialism which has come to be recognized in recent years is the extent to which the working group in factory or office does in fact provide this sort of fellowship. For many men and women the greatest satisfaction which their daily work gives them directly is that of participation in the friendship and common life of this group. At the same time there are also many arbitrary and depersonalizing relationships in modern industry which do violence to fellowship. This is especially true in the sphere of the exercise of authority and is largely a function of the scale of modern industry, which makes personal relationships impossible except in restricted fields.

(iii) *A common purpose.*

Underlying the needs for both creative opportunity and fellowship is the need for a common purpose. We have said all along that man is intended to exercise his creative powers and to co-operate with his neighbours to the glory of God, and that the essential purpose of the economic order is the glorifying of God and the doing of His Will. Therefore if economic activities are to be satisfying and purposeful and to produce true fellowship, they must be felt to have a common aim which is an expression in economic terms of God's Will for His people. This is bound up with what was said in the previous chapter about incentives. We saw there that the motive of self-interest was not enough. A healthy society is one which feels itself to have an ideal or aim that is shared by all and which calls forth the loyalty of its members in such a way that they are able to make their individual contributions fully and freely as persons.

The economic order tends to suffer because such a common purpose is usually lacking, except in times of unusual stress and danger, such as wartime. It is easier, however, to say that there should be a common purpose than to say what it should be. It is a question that is wider than the purely economic sphere, for it concerns the whole purpose of society, what society is conceived to be for. Our beliefs concerning the Will of God for society must find expression in a philosophy of society which finds general acceptance and can inspire human loyalty. In this connection the problem always arises of the relationship between the ideal of individual freedom and the ideal of individual loyalty to the community. In purely human terms we must assert that individual persons come first, and that wider communities consist of such persons and exist for their benefit. In economic terms, this means that the enjoyment by the individual members of the community of that flow of goods and services which gives them the fullest satisfaction comes first, and that the economic welfare of the community is only a means to this end. But man is not an isolated individual; he is a person who can only develop to the fullness of what he is intended to be as a member of a community, in fellowship with his neighbours and in the service of God. Therefore the fullest satisfaction of individuals calls in many cases for the subordination of the immediate interests of some members of the community to the wider interests of all, or a greater number, of the members. But this subordination must as far as possible be a willing and accepted one; hence the need for a commonly accepted ideal or purpose.

Two more detailed criteria by which the economic order can be judged may be mentioned briefly. They are really particular applications of the standards of economic efficiency and human efficiency.

C. Providing for stable and flexible progress.

An economic order may be judged by the extent by which it provides, not only for progress, but for stable and flexible progress. It is not enough that, over the long period, the trend is towards an increase of economic wealth relative to the population, important though that is. It is important also that this progress should be steady, that it should not take the form of violent fluctuations between prosperity and depression, between expansion and stagnation. Such fluctuations cause great waste of resources and much human suffering. It is important also that progress should be flexible. The system should be capable of adapting itself to meet unforeseen needs, or external shocks such as war or revolution, and it should be capable of making rapid use of new inventions and discoveries, without undue waste of resources engaged in existing forms of production. In other words, this criterion is concerned with the extent of the waste and dislocation involved in the process of economic development.

D. Avoiding the dangers of gross inequality of opportunity and of undue concentration of power.

An economic order may also be judged by the extent to which it combines economic efficiency with social justice. In particular, by how far it is able to combine a highly organized, efficient and flexible use of productive resources with an avoidance of the social defects of gross inequality of income and opportunity and of undue concentration of irresponsible economic power into a few hands. In other words, does the way in which it solves the problem of distribution, both of income and of power, conflict in its results in terms of welfare with the way in which it solves the problem of production?

Having established these criteria of the effectiveness of an economic system to fulfil the purposes for which it is intended, we shall be able in the next chapter to proceed to apply them to the economic order as we know it in the western world to-day.

CHAPTER FIVE

THE ECONOMIC ORDER AS
WE HAVE KNOWN IT

1. The Characteristics of the Free Enterprise Economy.

The economic system as we have known it in the western world
in the past two hundred years has had two main characteristics.
Technically it has been characterized by the increasing application of scientific knowledge in all its forms to the improvement
of productivity, notably by the use of mechanical power, and
by the application of chemical and biological analysis. In the
field of organization it has been characterized, at any rate in its
earlier and more formative days, by a reliance on the free enterprise of business men and industrialists regulated and inspired
by the pursuit of profit. It is therefore appropriate to refer to
it as a Free Enterprise Economy, in that free enterprise by
individual firms, rather than a conscious planning of the use of
resources by the community as a whole, was a dominant feature
of it. This is broadly true though even at the height of *laissez-
faire* it was admitted that there was a role in the economic
sphere for some conscious planning as exercised by the State.
As time went on, as we shall see, this role came to be greatly
extended, and the nature of the private sector of the economy
has also changed, in the direction of larger-scale organization.
Nevertheless, it is still by and large true to speak of a free
enterprise economy, even where it has come to function within
a framework of some degree of overall State planning.

In order to get a clearer picture of the nature of such an
economy, it will be helpful to begin by considering the way

in which the five main aspects of the economic problem mentioned in the last chapter are tackled under free enterprise. After this it will be possible to assess the achievements and limitations of the system.

A. Free exercise of effective demand in the market.

Essentially the demand problem, the problem of which wants are to be satisfied, is solved under free enterprise by the free exercise of effective demand in the market. By this we mean that what is produced depends ultimately upon the choices of income-receivers of how they are going to divide their command over goods and services between alternative uses so as to obtain the greatest satisfaction. There are two limitations. First of all, as we have seen, the types of goods and services which are in fact available, and the terms on which they are available, depend largely on the conditions of supply. It is, however, also true that the conditions of demand in turn react on supply, so that an increase of supply is stimulated to markets where demand is expanding, and supply discouraged to those where it is contracting. For instance, the demand for new goods like motor-cars and vacuum cleaners had to be created by the manufacturers of them. As it became technically possible to produce them more cheaply, so the demand for them spread more widely, but in turn the growth of demand stimulated cheaper production of the models which the public tended to want most. In this sense we can truly say that demand is ultimately prior to supply, but the range of choices open to the individual consumer in the short period is nevertheless usually limited to what the producers make available. Moreover, it is possible for the producers, by the use of advertising, considerably to influence consumers' wants and so induce a demand for the goods which they produce. Much popular demand for such things as toilet preparations, processed foods and patent-medicine is of this sort.

Secondly, it is effective demand, demand which is in a position to back itself with purchasing power, rather than need, which determines what is produced. This in turn depends on the distribution of income, so that where this is very unequal the luxuries of the rich may take precedence over the necessities of the poor.

Nevertheless the principle of consumers' sovereignty, or the determination of what shall be produced by the free exercise of demand by the consumers, finds general acceptance as the ultimate basis of any form of economic organization. It is the most efficient, since it avoids the inevitable waste involved in deciding what is to be produced by any other means, when it may turn out not to be wanted after all. It also corresponds to the purpose for which economic activity is undertaken, namely to enable people to satisfy their wants. In general, it is a sound principle that people themselves know best what they want and will get it most satisfactorily by choosing freely for themselves, and this corresponds to that dignity and freedom with which God has endowed all His children. In practice certain modifications have come to be accepted. Thus the Government, acting on behalf of the community, feels justified in prohibiting the production and sale of certain kinds of goods, such as dangerous drugs, and restricting that of others, such as alcoholic beverages. It also feels justified in limiting the free consumption of certain essential goods at times when they are felt to be scarce relative to the demand, e.g. by rationing and allocation. It also undertakes to supply free or below cost price, out of taxation, certain other types of services which are felt to be socially necessary or desirable, such as defence, law and order and the social services. These are, however, only exceptional modifications of the ultimate principle of consumers' sovereignty.

B. Competitive production under the stimulus of profit.

Production of goods and services is carried out in response to changes in demand, as expressed in market prices. The organization of production is carried out under free enterprise by the functionary whom the economists call 'the entrepreneur'—

the man who takes the risks of enterprise. Originally he was usually a single trader or industrialist; nowadays he is more usually a corporate body, the management of a limited company. The entrepreneur, individual or corporate, obtains his supplies of the factors of production, such as labour, raw materials, capital and land, by buying them in the market. He pays their owners fixed money prices, rates of wages or rates of interest, and himself gains the profits or bears the loss on what he decides to make and sell.

The regulating factor on which reliance is placed to secure the most economical use of resources is the force of competition, in the markets for both factors of production and products. The proportion in which the entrepreneur uses different types of labour or capital depends on the price he has to pay for them, which in turn depends on the price which their owners can obtain for them in other uses. Similarly, the type and quantities of products which the entrepreneur will make depend on the prices at which he can sell them, relative to the cost of making them. If competition is effective in the various markets, prices of factors and products will reflect closely the changes in the supply of them and the demand for them, for, if buyers and sellers are numerous, price cannot be artificially influenced by the actions of one or two of them. In such circumstances the actions of entrepreneurs, in seeking to maximize their profits by the way in which they combine the various types of factors to produce different types and quantities of products, will tend to ensure the most economical use of resources. Those goods will tend to be produced in larger quantities, for which demand, and hence price, is increasing, while the production of those for which demand, and price, is falling, will become less profitable and will tend to be cut down. If people want more television sets and less clothing, then, ideally, profits in the radio industry will rise and profits in the textile and clothing industries will fall, and competition will tend to bring about a switch of productive resources from the one to the other. Factors will tend to be used in those forms of production in which they bring the highest return, and the entrepreneur, seeking to minimize his costs relative to his output, will be driven by the price which he has to pay for them to adopt that combination of factors which is most economical. If the textile manufacturer finds that his labour can earn more in light engineering, then he will be driven by competition to use more machines and fewer men (or women); otherwise he will lose money.

The chief limitation of the economy of free enterprise production is the fact that competition is by no means always effective in the markets either for factors or for products. Control over the price of factors can often be exercised, either by the buyers or the sellers, or both. This is true in the case of many raw materials at any rate at particular times and places. It is even more true in the case of labour where bilateral bargaining between organized trade unions and employers' associations has largely replaced the free play of the market. This has arisen largely because without it the individual worker was usually in a very unfavourable bargaining position in relation to his employer, but also because the wage of labour is to its recipient much more than the mere market price of the factor which he sells. It is the livelihood on which he depends, and he naturally comes to value and to seek the security which can only be achieved by organization. The result, however, is a certain rigidity of wage structure which sometimes impedes the free flow of labour into those uses where it could be most economically employed. For this reason, as well as because of lack of training and unwillingness to move their homes and change their habits, displaced textile workers, for instance, do not move freely into engineering.

In the market for products, control over the price is more frequently exercised by the supplier than by the consumer, at any rate in the case of final consumption goods. In many cases producers, individually or collectively, can exercise a considerable control over the price they receive, by varying the quantity or quality which they supply. Therefore the output or quality of goods which they find it most profitable to produce, and hence the use of factors which they find it most profitable to make, may not be that which the consumers would choose under competitive conditions. In this connection we should remember that the distinction between the markets for factors and for products is to some extent an arbitrary one, since what are products to the producer at an earlier stage in the process become factors to those at later stages. The effects, therefore, of the existence of some degree of monopoly tend to be cumulative.

The problem of the reduction of effective competition tends to become more acute as the scale of production increases. Productive units tend to become larger, in order to be able to exploit the economies of scale, and therefore the number of producers tends to become smaller, and active competition between them tends to give way to varying degrees of tacit or open agreement. The problem of monopoly, and the weakening of the regulating force of competition, is therefore one of the prices which have to be paid for the benefits of increasing returns. One result of this is a growing tendency for the political organs of the community to intervene in the economic sphere, in the attempt to promote or provide by administrative action the guarantee of efficiency and protection to the consumer which the unfettered exercise of free enterprise shows signs of failing to provide. We shall be saying more about these developments later.

> c. Exchange in accordance with free market prices, depending on the interaction of supply and demand.

The terms on which the various types of goods and services are exchanged one against another depends upon the interaction of demand and supply in the market. The price level acts as the regulator to equate supply and demand. If demand is increased relative to supply (or supply is reduced relative to demand), price tends to rise, and this discourages an increase of supply, thus tending towards the restoration of equilibrium. Similarly if demand falls off relative to supply (or supply is increased relative to demand), price tends to fall and demand is stimulated and supply discouraged. The ease with which these adjustments take place depends upon the relative elasticities of demand and supply; that is, on the proportionate extent to which demand and supply are responsive to small changes in price.

Where a small change of price produces a proportionately larger change in the quantity of the goods demanded or supplied, demand or supply is said to be elastic. Where on the other hand the change in the quantity demanded or supplied is less than proportionate to the change in price, demand or supply is said to be inelastic.

The price mechanism is generally accepted as being the most effective regulator of supply and demand, since it works automatically with little friction and is sensitive and flexible in the face of changing conditions. This is especially true where there is a large number both of buyers and sellers, so that individuals have little direct control over price. Any dissatisfaction with its working which has been expressed on grounds of social justice has usually been directed against the effects of the unequal distribution of incomes rather than against the price mechanism itself. The chief cases where it has been found necessary to modify its operation are those where both supply and demand are highly inelastic in the short period, and where either of them has undergone a sudden and violent change, to which this inelasticity prevents easy adaptation. The best examples are connected with the demand for the production of war supplies and with variations in the supply of basic foodstuffs and raw materials. In the case of war production or large-scale rearmament we have a sudden, violent and highly inelastic[1] increase

---

[1] i.e. an increase which would not be choked off even by a considerable rise in price.

of demand for certain types of goods and services. It is not possible to rely on an increase of market prices to induce the necessary supply. The Government cannot depend on a rise in the market price of guns and an increase in the profits of the armament manufacturers to secure that they produce the munitions needed, but must have recourse to direct control of the necessary production and of the supplies of essential materials and labour. Under the stress of wartime needs and stringencies, the principle of the control of prices and production came to be extended much more widely, until the free working of the price mechanism came to be largely suspended. In the case of basic foodstuffs and materials, in times of acute shortage, such as war and post-war periods, the allocation of these between different uses cannot be left to follow the bidding-up of prices without causing undue hardship, and rationing and allocation schemes and price controls are therefore adopted. If, on the other hand, there is a glut of them, relative to demand, as in the 1930's, the governments of producing countries are led to adopt schemes of output restriction and subsidized price maintenance in order to prevent the hardship among the producers concerned which is caused by the resultant severe slump of prices.

D. Income distribution according to the market value of the services of the factors concerned.

The distribution of incomes under the free-enterprise system is in general determined by the market value of the services of the factors controlled by the recipients. Thus wage rates and salary scales depend upon the market value of the services of the type of human skill and experience concerned. Similarly with incomes received in the form of interest and dividends on capital and rent of land, and with the profits which are the reward of the enterprise of the entrepreneur.

Since it is the market value of the services, as determined by effective supply and demand, on which relative incomes depend, it follows that the distribution of incomes is very un-equal. The supply of those types of labour, for instance, which require little skill or training, is normally high relative to the demand, so that unskilled labour commands low wages, even though it may involve arduous or unpleasant conditions. More highly skilled labour and professional services, requiring greater training and experience, and usually greater natural ability, have a greater scarcity value[1] and therefore command a higher return. The possessors of rare natural gifts for which there happens to be a great demand, such as those of Q.C.s and film stars, can often command an even higher return. A greater source of inequality of income than unequal earning power is the un-equal ownership of property, which is intensified by inheritance. Not only does it cause inequality directly through the concen-tration of income from the services of capital into comparatively few hands, it also intensifies the inequality of earning power, since the children of the well-to-do have greater opportunities of acquiring the necessary training and skills than have those of the less well-off.

The main remedy against the inequality of incomes has been the system of progressive taxation and social services developed by the Government. By progressive income-tax and surtax the advantage in purchasing power of the receivers of large incomes is greatly reduced, and by the death duties the worst effects of inheritance on inequality of property ownership are mitigated. Out of the proceeds of taxation the State can do something to alleviate inequality of opportunity by providing free or subsidized education, health services, housing and other social services. Another effective remedy has been the development of col-lective bargaining, and its extension, with State support, to cover the less skilled workers. This problem of inequality of incomes will be dealt with more fully in a later section of this chapter.

[1] This scarcity value is to some extent artificial, owing to limited educational opportunities.

D

E. Savings determined by expectations of income-receivers; investment by those of entrepreneurs. The rate of interest as the regulating factor.

The level of saving under free enterprise is determined by the expectations of income-receivers, both individual and corporate. Those who receive individual incomes decide what proportion of them they will set aside from present consumption, according to what they can spare out of their incomes, according to their desire to make provision for old age or other contingencies, according to their estimates of the possibilities of finding a profitable outlet for their savings, or on similar grounds. Nowadays an increasing proportion of the community's saving is done corporately, largely through the undistributed profits of companies, and the level of these is determined by expectations as to the future prospects and capital needs of the businesses concerned.

The level of investment, on the other hand, depends upon the entrepreneurs' expectations as to the return on the capital invested, relative to the cost of borrowing it, and that depends on estimates of the future course of business, both in the industry or trade concerned and in the economy in general.

Thus it is income-receivers, individual and corporate, who decide how much of the community's flow of goods and services it is intended shall be consumed in any given period, and how much is to be set aside through saving. It is entrepreneurs, on the other hand, who decide how much of the community's resources shall be invested in maintaining or extending its productive capacity, in the form of new buildings, machines, plant and stocks. The regulating factor is the rate of interest, which is both the reward for withholding resources from consumption and making them available for investment, and the price which entrepreneurs have to pay to secure the use of capital for investment. Ideally, therefore, and in the long period, the rate of interest acts as a market price equating the supply of capital with the demand for it and allocating the available capital resources between alternative uses.

This is one of the spheres in which our economy is apt to act least smoothly. In the short period the rate of interest exercises relatively little influence on the volume either of saving or investment. How much people try to save depends much more on the level of their incomes and on their beliefs about future movements of prices. People normally tend to save more, for instance, when their incomes increase, but if they expect prices to rise in the future, they may prefer to spend the extra income here and now. In either case the level of the rate of interest will not affect them very greatly. How much entrepreneurs try to invest depends much more on what the expected return on the investment is likely to be than on the price which they have to pay for borrowed capital, which is usually only a minor element in costs. A firm contemplating putting a lot of new machinery into a factory will be influenced more by the profits it hopes to make by using the new plant, than by the rate of interest it has to pay on the borrowed capital necessary to install it.

Therefore it is easy for attempted saving and attempted investment to get out of step and the result is a disorder of the economic system. The attempt of the community to save more than it invests leads to a deficiency of effective demand, because the excess savings involve a withdrawal of income from consumption which is not balanced by the making of purchasing power available through investment. The result is a general depression of trade and widespread unemployment, until the making of losses wipes out the attempted excess saving, and savings and investment are equated at a level at which productive capacity is seriously under-employed. The attempt of the community to invest more than it saves leads to a diversion of resources from the production of consumption-goods to the production of investment-goods, which is not balanced by a withdrawal of income from consumption demand. The extra demand from income-receivers which results from the investment, pressing on the inadequate resources of consumption goods, leads to a forcing up of prices. Consumption is thus reduced by a process of 'forced saving', and this process of inflation will tend to continue until saving and investment are brought into balance.

As a result of the Great Depression of 1929-32 and of the war-time and post-war experiences of inflationary pressure, it has come to be accepted that the Government has the responsibility of holding the balance between saving and investment. This it should do by adjusting its own revenue-raising and spending activities, so as to offset a deficiency of saving by increased taxation and a Budget surplus, or a deficiency of investment by increased spending and a Budget deficit. By so doing it not only stimulates saving or investment, as the case may be, by its own direct action, but also indirectly, by influencing consumption. A reduction of taxation and an increase of Government spending will tend to bring about increased consumption by income-receivers, especially if the spending takes the form of social services designed to bring about a more equal distribution of incomes. Similarly, an increase of taxation and a reduction of Government spending will have the reverse effect. In effect the Government undertakes itself to do the necessary saving or investment, which the community is unwilling to do for itself. Such a policy has worked moderately well as a means of controlling inflationary pressure in post-war years. Its effectiveness against the onset of a world-wide depression has still to be tested. One difficulty would be the extent to which each national economy is dependent on the course of events outside its own boundaries, and hence not susceptible to the control of individual governments. The experience of 1929-32 suggests that some degree of international co-operation would be essential.

Having surveyed some of the chief distinctive characteristics of the free enterprise economy, as shown by the way in which the main aspects of the economic problem are tackled under it, we can now proceed to assess some of its achievements and limitations.

2. Its achievements.

A. The great increase of economic wealth over the past two hundred years.

In its main task of bringing about an increase of economic wealth, the economic system as we have known it has undoubtedly been successful. In the countries of western Europe, North America and Australasia, and the others which have been most directly affected, the development of mechanical industry and the opening up of the world through improved communications have meant an increase of wealth which has far outstripped the great increase of population which has accompanied it. It is true that inequality of incomes has continued, and has been checked by political and social measures rather than by purely economic means. Nevertheless, the standard of living of the ordinary family in the western world to-day is immensely higher than it was at the beginning of last century. The increased flow of goods and services made possible by modern industry and transport, and the increasing application of scientific knowledge, has brought benefits in the form of better food, better housing, better clothing and greater amenities, which are enjoyed by all, even if some enjoy more of them than others.

It is true that this benefit has accrued mainly to those countries which have been the chief centres of mechanized industry and large-scale commerce, and to the newly-settled countries which have been able to develop large-scale agriculture. Outside western Europe, North America and Australasia, the fruits of western technical achievement have tended to be enjoyed mainly by a small ruling class, and the bulk of the people have remained in their traditional poverty. This is one of the facts which have given such an impetus to Communism in the under-developed areas in recent years. It must be remembered also that much of the wealth of the west has been made possible by its access to the resources of the rest of the world, and in particular the existence of the vast areas of virgin land waiting to be opened up by western capital and immigration. Nevertheless, it was under the free enterprise economy that this double process of industrialization and colonization took place, and mechanized industry and commerce have at least opened the way to the possibility of increased economic wealth for other countries also. By means of large-scale industry and the introduction of capital from more developed countries, it is possible both to develop the natural resources of the poorer countries more fully, and to ease the pressure of the population on the land. Absorption of labour into industry makes possible a more efficient agriculture with a smaller labour force, because the use of more modern methods increases the productivity of labour in agriculture. The main difficulty is the rapid increase of population which any improvement of conditions brings with it, and which is no longer offset, as it was in Europe last century, by the rapid opening up of virgin lands.

Economically, therefore, we must say that our system has been a great success. It has been very successful in making a more economical use of the world's natural resources and of man's talents to make available a greatly increased flow of goods and services for man's satisfaction. This is true in spite of the waste of resources which has sometimes accompanied it, in the reckless exhaustion of mineral resources, the cutting down of forests and the over-exploiting of the fertility of newly cultivated soil. Socially it has been less successful. Though making possible a great increase of wealth and of the standard of living, it has not succeeded in the same way in bringing about an increase in true satisfaction, a greater sense of the purpose and worth-whileness of life. In particular, it has not been able to capture the imagination and active loyalty of the bulk of the industrial wage-earners. They have not come to feel that they have a part and share in the system, that it is a co-operative effort for the

54

common good. Men have in fact come to be more and more dependent on each other's efforts, but they have not been made to feel this. Rather there has grown up a sense of antagonism between employees and managements, a sense of exploitation on the one side and of recalcitrance on the other. The doctrine of 'Class War' owes its theoretical origin to the sociology of Marx, but it would not have won the power which it has exercised over the minds of men had it not corresponded to something real in their felt experiences. Our analysis of some of the defects and shortcomings of the Free Enterprise System will perhaps throw some light on the reasons for this.

B. These successes are largely the fruits of the virtues of free enterprise.

The successes of our economic system in tackling the problem of production so efficiently are largely the fruits of the free enterprise which on the whole has characterized it. Before going on therefore to consider some of the disadvantages and limitations which the system has also manifested, it will be as well to list some of the strong points of free enterprise.

(i) *Scope for enterprise and initiative in new developments.*

The first and most obvious advantage of a system which depends for its motive power on the free activity of individuals rewarded by profits is the undoubted scope which it gives for enterprise and initiative in new developments. Those who have the wisdom to see the opportunities for the development of new processes or products, or for the opening up of new markets, find few legal or institutional obstacles in their way. If they have the energy and perseverance to follow them up, they have the chance of reaping their reward in handsome profits. Those who choose wrongly are penalized by heavy losses. Most of the formative developments in modern industry and commerce were the fruits of the vision and energy of a few individuals. This has been true even in more recent years, when the supply of capital has come to be in the hands of large-scale companies rather than of single entrepreneurs, but on the whole there is probably a greater chance of such opportunities being fully taken in a system which gives room for the man with the vision to back his own ideas than in one where all progress depends upon his being able to persuade the bureaucracy of a huge and cumbersome organization.

(ii) *Enlistment of the self-regarding element in man in the service of more efficient production.*

A system of free enterprise regulated by profit has a further advantage in that it affords the maximum opportunity for enlisting the self-regarding element in man in the service of more efficient production. We have already seen that this is probably the strongest motive to economic activity. A system which provides that those who show enterprise and initiative in making available to people what they are willing to buy reap the full reward in terms of profit, undoubtedly provides a stronger incentive power than one in which the material rewards are less directly connected with successful effort. Similarly, the penalizing of false economic choices by the making of losses acts as an incentive towards an efficient use of resources. The effect, however, is a tendency to promote productive efficiency at the expense of inequality of incomes.

(iii) *Scope for creative self-expression.*

Not only does free enterprise encourage the seizing of opportunities for economic development, it also provides scope for creative self-expression on the part of those who undertake them. We have already seen that man's creative powers are a gift from his Creator, to be used to the full in co-operation with Him. These creative powers are best exercised by some men in the development of new means to satisfy men's wants more effectively. There is obviously greater scope for this if there is opportunity for those who have the vision to build up businesses for themselves in which this vision can find expression. It is true that, owing to human frailty, the results may not always be in accordance with the Will of God, but without taking such risks, creativeness is severely hampered. The community has the right and the duty, however, of exercising some sort of supervision over the results. It is true also that it takes more than creative vision to build up a business or exploit a new process; it takes capital also, and the two do not always go together. Many developments which might have been of benefit to man must have been neglected or delayed because those who had the ideas could not secure the capital.

(iv) *Economic freedom as a buttress of social political freedom.*

Economic freedom, in the sense of a fairly wide diffusion of economic power and opportunity, acts as a buttress to social and political freedom. One of the dangers of the Totalitarian State is that it tends to concentrate all form of power, social, political and economic, into the hands of the dominant group. It may be argued that the dangers of totalitarianism through political power or social pressure are lessened when economic power is well diffused. Men can exercise their independence of pressures from political interests more successfully if they are not dependent on them for their livelihood. Undoubtedly the concentration of control over employment and the ownership of the means of production into the hands of the political organs of the State involve grave dangers, unless these are recognized and adequate steps taken to ensure autonomy and independence by other means. This is one of the problems of Democratic Socialism to which its supporters have not yet given sufficient attention. It will be discussed more fully later, when we come to consider Planning as an alternative to free enterprise.

57

(v) *The Free Enterprise System is largely self-regulating.*

Because the free enterprise system depends for its motive power on the interacting decisions of individual producers and consumers, it is largely self-regulating in its operation. The choices which govern the level and nature of economic activity, how much of each type of goods and services should be produced, how much investment in capital goods should take place and in what directions, what should be the level of prices and the distribution of incomes, are not made deliberately of any body of people acting for the community as a whole, but are the resultants of the choices of individuals concerning how they will get and spend their living. The co-ordination of these individual choices is carried out through the price mechanism. In each market, whether it is for various types of consumption goods, or for producers' goods such as raw materials, or for labour or capital, a shortage of supply relative to demand provokes a rise in price, and a falling short of demand relative to supply provokes a fall in price. These price movements in turn stimulate counteracting changes in supply and demand.

Ideally, therefore, the free enterprise system has a high degree of flexibility and adaptability. A miscalculation in one direction, an over- or under-estimate, say by producers, of the demand for some particular product, should quickly provoke the appropriate change in price levels and thus bring about corrective movements. An increase of demand in one direction, or a falling off in another, should quickly bring about adjustments on the part of producers. Changes in conditions of production, making certain types of goods cheaper or more costly to produce, should similarly promote corresponding increases or decreases of demand. In practice, of course, as we shall see, this flexibility is by no means as complete or as satisfactory in its results as it is in free enterprise theory. Nevertheless, flexibility and adaptability and a certain degree of automatic adjustment remain characteristics of a relatively 'free' system as opposed to a largely 'planned' one.

3. *Its defects and dangers.*

Against the successes of our economic system in tackling the problem of production, and the virtues of free enterprise in promoting economic efficiency and political freedom, must be set some striking defects and dangers. These limitations have led, in the ways which we shall see, to a great extension in the scope of the responsibilities undertaken by the State in the economic field and to the growth of the idea of planning as a possible alternative to free enterprise. Most of them we have already met in our consideration of the way in which the different economic functions are performed under free enterprise, but in order to get a clearer picture it will be necessary to summarize them and enlarge on them.

A. The tendency towards inequality of income and opportunity.

In the first place, reliance on the free following of the profit motive inevitably brings with it a tendency towards cumulative inequality of income, opportunity and economic power. In order to understand this, and the part played by free enterprise in it, it will be necessary to examine the role of inequality in the economic order in more detail.

(i) *A certain degree of inequality is inevitable as a result of men's unequal talents.*

Inequality is in itself inherent in the economic order, as in any other aspect of human activity, since it is a reflection of the inequality of men's gifts and talents. In the Christian view, all men are of equal and infinite value in the sight of God, but they are not equal in the sense of being identical. Each is a unique personality, each has his varying gifts and talents, and each has his own contribution to make. It therefore follows that some men are by nature more fitted for success in the organizing of economic affairs than others, and some are more adapted for success in the acquiring of wealth and power than others, should they be so minded. Moreover, in the functioning of a complex economic system, as in any other form of corporate activity, some men must undoubtedly exercise greater responsibility and greater authority than others.

A certain degree of inequality, in power, responsibility, and in command over goods and services, is therefore inevitable in the economic system. This is the more true, because reliance is placed on the incentive of material reward to get the world's work done. Therefore those types of work which call for greater responsibility or longer training, or for which for any reason the supply of labour is scarce relative to the demand, must offer a higher return, in money and other advantages, to attract suitable people to do them. This is true not so much because men need the inducement of money to make them willing to exercise responsibility or undertake training, but because higher earnings have become the accepted symbol of the social prestige which goes with a more responsible position, and because such persons are able to command such an extra reward in return for making their services available. Inequality in this sense is a reflection of difference of function, modified to take account of man's fallen nature and the strength of the self-regarding motive. The safeguard against the dangers of too great inequality must be an active consciousness of the fact that men, though unequal in this sense, are equal in the deeper sense of being all equally children of God and uniquely precious in His sight. The responsibility for securing that such a consciousness is active rests on Christians and must form part of their social and economic witness.

(ii) *Our economic system unduly accentuates and encourages inequality.*

The defect of our economic system, then, is not that inequalities of income, opportunity and power exist under it, but that these are excessive. They have been pushed beyond the stage when they reflect approximately the necessary diversity of functions and have reached a point where they are a serious danger to the realization of that sense of neighbourliness and brotherhood which is God's intention for His children. This is nothing new in the history of man and is in no sense the creation of modern industrialism; it has existed ever since civilization began. The increase of wealth which accompanied man's rise from a state of savagery has always gone along with a great inequality in its distribution. The great increase in productivity which modern industrialism has brought does, however, serve to make more glaring the great contrasts between wealth and poverty which still exist in the world, in spite of the general rise of living standards. Now that it is within man's power to produce so much more, there is felt to be less excuse for distributing the fruits so unequally. We are no longer willing, as our fathers were, to accept 'the rich man in his castle, the poor man at his gate' as part of the divinely decreed order of things. In recent years the western world has indeed seen considerable progress towards greater equality, not least in Britain, but this has been achieved by deliberate political action rather than by the free working of the economic system.

Such inequality is in fact the inevitable consequence of a reliance on individual enterprise motivated mainly by the pursuit of material reward. If the profit incentive is to be effective, the profits which those who are successful in enterprise can secure must be considerable; the bigger the prize, the greater the incentive. Although failure of judgment may be penalized by equally heavy losses, yet on the whole the acquisition of wealth tends to be cumulative. Those who have a certain amount of capital behind them are in a better position to exploit further opportunities; money tends to breed money, as the saying is. They can also give their children better opportunities for securing the capital necessary to start in a favourable position in their turn, and the training that will enable them to compete for the well-paid jobs. By inheritance, moreover, their children are left both with a source of income from the ownership of property, and with the necessary capital to form the basis for the further increase of wealth. It is true this tendency for wealth to accumulate is in time often offset by reckless spending or lack of business sense or other misfortune on the part of future generations, so that fortunes can disappear as well as be built up. The tendency is there, nevertheless, and in the short run, at any rate, fortunes tend to grow rather than to decline, in the absence of external factors such as discriminatory taxation.

The reliance on the incentive of profit thus causes a cumulative tendency towards greater inequality of incomes and hence of opportunities. The free enterprise system has also tended to encourage inequality through its reliance on the accumulated resources of the well-to-do as a source of capital. A more unequal distribution of incomes seems on the whole to bring about a greater volume of saving, since a small minority of well-to-do people are apt to have a larger surplus over and above what they want to spend on consumption. Where incomes are more equally distributed, the likelihood is that any surplus will go mainly on increased consumption rather than on saving. In its formative days, the modern industrial system relied mainly on individual savings, at first those of entrepreneurs engaged directly in industry themselves, and later those of investors with a surplus of private means who wanted a bit of extra income from them. More recently, with the growth of taxation, the tendency has been to rely less on private savings and more on the corporate savings of industry itself, in the form of undistributed profits, and on the surpluses of the public authorities.[1]

[1] The Government publication, *National Income and Expenditure, 1946-51*, indicates that, in 1951, personal savings accounted for only some 7 per cent of total savings, whereas corporate saving accounted for 53 per cent, and government surpluses for 40 per cent.

(iii) *Gross inequality is a barrier to fellowship.*

Extreme inequality of income and opportunity is a barrier to that sense of fellowship which we have seen to be inherent in God's purposes for the economic order. Where the gap in the standard of living is very great between the different income-groups, there is a gap in understanding also. People whose ways of life are very different tend to have little in common and to have difficulty in understanding one another. In ideas and habits of thought and action, and even in speech, they do not speak the same language. One finds something like Disraeli's 'two nations' arising.

Not only is there a gap in understanding, there may also be a sense of antagonism. Where different classes are obviously getting very different relative shares of the product of the economic order in which they are all involved, and shares which do not appear to be commensurate with the differences in effort contributed, it is obvious that class differences will be accentuated. The essence of social class is something more complex than difference of income level or economic function, it is true, and the Marxist theory is an over-simplification, but an obvious clash of economic interests has its effects nevertheless. Those who feel that they are not getting their fair share become resentful and feel they are being exploited, while those who feel that their present share is being endangered also become resentful and talk in terms of the need for subordination. Talk of the greed and laziness of the 'wicked capitalists' on the one side comes to be matched by talk of the laziness and incompetence of the 'common working man' on the other. This is an exaggerated picture of a danger which in a healthy society tends to be counteracted by common loyalties and shared experiences which make for greater understanding, but, where extremes of wealth and poverty are very great, the disruptive forces are very powerful.

(iv) *Does inequality lead to greater economic efficiency?*

It is doubtful whether such exaggerated inequality leads to any compensating increase of economic efficiency. The spur of profit and the incentive to increased earnings are certainly necessary to secure the fullest output of effort and the requisite mobility of labour, capital and enterprise. They are also needed to encourage the taking of responsibility and the undertaking of specialized training. But inequality carried to excess produces economic disadvantages. The sense of resentment and injustice which it breeds may stultify much enterprise which would otherwise be fruitful. Lack of opportunity prevents the talents of many from being used to the fullest extent and thus results in the loss to the community of much valuable service. And if the inequality is such that the ordinary working man or peasant cannot achieve a reasonable share of the necessities and ordinary decencies of life for himself and his family, the actual efficiency of labour may suffer. Countries such as India and China, where the average income of the bulk of the people is very low, are also countries of low labour productivity. Moreover, in an economy in which income distribution became progressively more unequal, there would be a grave danger of eventual breakdown, through under-consumption and the failure of effective demand. As people's incomes increase, at any rate beyond a certain point, they tend to save an increasing proportion of them. Consequently, in a community where real income was increasing, but its distribution becoming more unequal, the tendency would be for consumption not to expand as fast as income. Therefore, unless investment was expanding fast enough to absorb the increased savings, there would be a danger of a failure of effective demand and a tendency towards depression and unemployment, because the purchasing power withdrawn from consumption in the form of savings would not be finding its way into demand for goods and services via investment.

(v) *Factors which have offset the tendency to inequality.*

If the tendency towards inequality were allowed to continue unchecked, therefore, it would have dangerous effects on economic efficiency, as well as on social welfare. Fortunately, the evolution of our social and political order has produced a number of counteracting tendencies.

In the first place, the development of administration, the professions and the service trades generally, has produced a great expansion of the middle classes, and particularly of the ranks of those who are paid fixed salaries. Since their remuneration is reasonably fixed, and since the work which they do is usually of greater intrinsic interest and social prestige, they are less directly concerned with the incentive of the pursuit of wealth. There has thus come to be a more regular gradation of income groups.

In the second place, the organization of the wage-earners into trade unions has greatly increased their bargaining power and has ensured that they have shared in the general increase of the community's income.

In the third place, the State has adopted the policy of counteracting income inequality by progressive taxation and the provision of social services to redress inequality of opportunity.

These factors between them have gone far, especially in recent years, to mitigate both the social and the economic consequences of inequality.

B. Irresponsible concentration of power.

Closely allied to the concentration of income and opportunity is the concentration of power. Power must of course be concentrated in any form of human organization. There must always be a comparatively small number of people whose responsibility it is in varying degrees to take decisions and give instructions, while the majority must carry them out. This is true in the

E

economic field once you get two or three men working together on any form of productive enterprise. It becomes increasingly true with the increase in the scale of production. As firms and factories become larger, effective economic power comes to be concentrated into fewer hands. The degree of power exercised by the management of a large modern firm is inevitably very great. It affects directly the livelihood and working conditions of large numbers of men and women, and also the conditions under which important products and services are made available to the community.

The criticism of the exercise of power in our modern economic system is concerned not so much with the fact of its exercise as with the fact that it is largely irresponsible. The management of the modern productive undertaking is vested typically in the board of directors of a joint-stock company, responsible nominally to the shareholders. The shareholders are usually a large and heterogeneous body with no real knowledge or concern for the welfare of the firm, except in so far as their dividends are affected. In practice, therefore, unless things go badly wrong, the management is effectively responsible to no one. The interests of the consumers are protected in theory by competition, but in many cases this is comparatively ineffective. The interests of the employees are protected ultimately by their union and by the right to strike, but this is a clumsy instrument and its use is itself a sign that responsible relations have broken down. Apart from these checks, the exercise of power by the management, over those who depend on it for their livelihood and over the community which depends on it for service is arbitrary. The power may in fact be well and conscientiously exercised, but it is nevertheless arbitrary.

A great deal of the dissatisfaction with the present-day organization of industry springs from this sense of the irresponsibility of the exercise of economic power. It is a problem for which a solution has yet to be found, for managements have the essential function of securing industrial efficiency and must have the necessary authority to do so. Any sort of representative democracy, such as is appropriate in the political sphere, would seem to be ruled out in the economic sphere. Yet an authority which is felt to be arbitrary will always be resented, and is always open to the danger of abuse. The problem is more acute than it was in the days of small-scale undertakings. Then, the exercise of authority within the firm was a matter of personal contacts, and personal respect and knowledge tended to season otherwise arbitrary relationships. The interests of the community as a whole were fairly well protected by competition. Nowadays, these mitigating factors are less in evidence. In the matter of working conditions, the development of joint consultation between managements and workers' representatives, with trade union co-operation, offers a prospect of some advance towards a solution, but it is still in an experimental stage.[1] On the side of the protection of the consumer, the problem merges into that of monopoly, which is treated later in this chapter.

c. Tendency to exalt the acquisitive instinct in man.

The two dangers we have dealt with are bound up with a third, a tendency to over-value and exalt the acquisitive element in man's nature. This is a natural result of the free enterprise system's success in harnessing the self-regarding instinct in the service of production. Because the gaining of material wealth is the reward for providing the goods and services for which people are willing to pay, it comes to be regarded as itself the chief sign of social success. To get rich comes to be valued as an end in itself, or as means to prestige and power, rather than as the reward for rendering services to the community. Inevitably the emphasis comes to be on the riches rather than on the

---

[1] The term 'joint consultation' has come to mean the establishment, especially at factory level, of consultative organizations representing management and workers, concerned not with wages and conditions but with such matters as improvement in methods of production and questions of safety, health and welfare. For an account of the movement, see Ministry of Labour—Industrial Relations Handbook—Supplement No. 3, December, 1949, entitled *Joint Consultation in Industry*.

service, and this is the more true in so far as the size of the reward is out of proportion to the real value of the services rendered. Many people have or acquire riches without appearing to make a commensurate contribution to society. Thus the possession of monetary wealth comes to acquire a semi-moral connotation. Those who are well-to-do and successful in making money come to be admired and treated with respect for that reason alone, while those who are less well-off and less successful in making money come to be regarded as inferior. 'Success,' in the sense of being in a position to command the material things of life, comes to be set up as an ideal to be striven after and achieved as the most worthwhile thing in life.

Such an attitude is usually implicit rather than explicit. Few probably would admit that they regarded wealth and position as the most important things in life, and most, if challenged, would probably agree that ultimately there were other things more important. That this is so is evidenced by the capacity for self-sacrifice and disinterested service of which so many show themselves to be capable, once their imagination is aroused. Yet in a society so organized that social esteem and wealth go together, and in which so many are engaged in a daily struggle to obtain more money or retain what they have, the whole climate of moral values comes to be directed towards the overestimation of wealth and of the acquisitive instinct.

Society is here in something of a dilemma. If economic wealth is to be increased, so that all may have a fair share, the world's productive resources must be effectively organized. Given human limitations, this means that it is essential that adequate material incentives to effort and responsibility should exist. If these are unduly curbed, so that those who have vision and take risks no longer reap what they feel to be an adequate reward, while those who fail to show enterprise and who waste resources are able to do equally well, the result is likely to be frustration and inefficiency. If free rein is given to the pursuit of profit and higher earnings, even when competition can be relied upon to secure that these forces work in the direction of economic efficiency, the result will nevertheless be an over-valuing of acquisitiveness.

One effect of this exaltation of self-seeking and this lack of a common purpose is a depersonalization of human relations. In a society in which personal material success is the accepted aim, there is a tendency to treat other people as instruments to be used for the achievement of one's own ends, rather than as persons to whom respect is due as fellow-children of God. Relationships in large-scale organizations such as those of modern industry and business must inevitably be impersonal, but this is mitigated if, behind the necessary impersonal planning, there is a realization that the men and women concerned are in fact persons and a determination to treat them as such, especially in one's direct contacts with them.

D. Instability—progress goes through cycles of prosperity and depression.

Economic progress has not only been accompanied by inequality in the distribution of its fruits, it has also been very unstable. Although over the long period there has been a persistent tendency towards an increase in the volume of goods and services becoming available, relative to the population, in the short period there have been violent fluctuations between prosperity and depression. In fact, over the past hundred and fifty years or so a regular succession of these alternations of boom and slump can be traced, to which we give the name of the trade cycle. The general characteristics of these fluctuations are well known. They are international in scope, spreading from one country to another through the inter-relations of trade and finance. They affect the whole economy, but capital goods industries are affected much more severely than consumption goods industries, and, in countries where international trade is especially important, export industries are affected more severely than home market industries. Consumers' services are usually affected the least of all. The incidence of the trade cycle can be deflected by external factors, such as the large-scale government spending which accompanies wars, but when no such factors operate the average length of each cycle is around eight to ten years, the depression phase being usually rather longer than the phase of prosperity.

There is no space here to go into the details of the causes of the trade cycle, about which economic theory has been busy for long enough. Suffice it to say that the root cause is generally recognized to lie in the lack of correlation between the level of attempted saving and that of attempted investment in the economy. The course of the cycle is usually something as follows.

An expansion of investment, the building of new factories, the installation of new machinery, and the building up of stocks of materials and goods in process, creates an expansion of incomes through the employment to which it gives rise. This leads to an expansion of demand for consumption goods by the income-receivers, and this in turn leads to a further expansion of the economy. This is aided by a general expansion of credit through the banking system. The result is general prosperity, rising prices, rising profits, little unemployment, a general atmosphere of optimism which encourages further expansion.

The upward process comes to an end for two possible reasons. The pressure of demand for skilled labour and for certain types of materials, increased overtime and the development of shortages, may lead to rising costs, which may outrun prices and cut into profits. At the same time, as people's incomes rise with the general prosperity, and especially as profits, individual and corporate, rise relative to wages and other more fixed incomes, there is a tendency towards increased saving, so that consumption does not continue to expand at the same rate, and expected profits are not made. Business men then begin to revise their plans and to cut down their investment in capital goods such as plant and machinery and allow their stocks to run down. This is encouraged by a more stringent credit policy being pursued by the monetary authorities, so that credit comes to be contracted. The reduction in investment causes a reduction in incomes and hence in demand and a cumulative down-swing sets in, with prices falling and losses being made. The economy goes into a depression. The losses eventually wipe out the excess saving which brought about the onset of the downward process. The up-swing begins again when business men begin cautiously to replenish stocks, or to instal new plant in order to reduce costs at a time of low prices. Once investment starts again, the whole process of expansion is set in motion again.

This instability of the system is extremely wasteful as well as causing much hardship. During the period of depression, a large proportion of the labour force may be out of work, some of them for years on end, and factories and plant are idle too. Farmers, whose output is less easily adapted to changes in demand, find that the prices which they get for their produce slump much more severely than the prices which they have to pay for manufactured goods. The Great Depression of 1929-32, coming on a world whose economy had not fully recovered from the dislocations of the first world war, brought about a virtual breakdown of the international system of free interchange of goods and services and free availability of foreign exchange to pay for them. Each country felt obliged to take steps to protect itself by means of tariffs, quotas, exchange controls and bilateral agreements.

During the period of prosperity, many unsound ventures are started. Owing to the easy profits being made by some, and the general atmosphere of incautious optimism, resources come to be locked up in enterprises where they prove to be wasted once the boom breaks. This is the more true if the monetary system is inadequately controlled, and credit is made available too freely. The typical nineteenth-century boom always culminated in an orgy of speculation in unsound ventures, followed by a financial crisis in which many people were ruined and confidence was badly shaken.

Psychologically and socially, the effects of instability are even more unfortunate. The sense of insecurity produced by the existence of widespread unemployment, the fear of losing one's job at any moment with little prospect of getting another one quickly, is most harmful both to the individual and to society as a whole. The actual experience of prolonged unemployment is still more harmful. A man comes to feel that he is not wanted; that there is no useful place for him in the community. Some instability and some unemployment there must always be, of course. Some occupations are always expanding and needing more labour, while others are contracting and needing less. There are always some men who want to move from one job to another. Where changes in the relative importance of different industries are on a large scale, they may cause a considerable problem of unemployment in the areas where the declining industries are located, because labour is relatively immobile. This is the more true where the declining industries are export industries, as was the case in Britain in the inter-war period, for the expanding industries which replace them may not be in the same country. We then get the problem of 'Depressed Areas'. Such structural unemployment, as it is called, along with the cyclical unemployment which arises in the depression stage of the trade cycle, together form the core of the problem of unemployment. It was the coincidence of the two of them, in Britain in the 1930's, which led to the gradual acceptance of the belief that the State has the responsibility of taking measures to prevent such drastic instability in the economy.

The fear of unemployment has also had serious adverse effects on economic efficiency through its impact on the minds of those who have suffered from it. It is the main reason for the insistence by trade unionists on the maintenance of restrictive practices, such as strict apprenticeship requirements for craftsmen, the demarcation of the work to be done by different trades, and the fear of the redundancy which may be caused by the use of improved methods. Similar effects on the thinking of business men lead to a desire for price-fixing and output restriction and opposition to new processes. Even the experience of more than ten years of full employment has not succeeded in removing altogether the fear that some day there will be another depression, and consequently, at a time when increased productivity is urgently needed, it is hampered by the psychological effects of unemployment.

The element of instability in the economic system, therefore, and especially its liability to periodic breakdown into general depression, has been one of the strongest factors in leading to an extension of the economic responsibilities of the State. The acceptance of this responsibility has been hastened by the parallel duty, arising out of the needs of wartime and post-war government spending, to avoid the opposite danger of general inflation.

E. Wastefulness—waste of natural resources, human ability, and capital. The conflict between social and private advantage.

The progress which has been achieved by our economic system has been a prodigal one. It has taken place at the expense of considerable waste of natural resources, human abilities and capital. Natural resources have been wasted by short-sighted exploitation with too little thought for the future. Forests have been cut down without replanting, irreplaceable mineral resources have been worked with little thought for economy, and quickly exhausted.[1] The fertility of virgin soils has been exhausted by over-cropping and the cultivation of marginal land, and dust bowls have been created in the process. In industrial development, amenity has been sacrificed to quick returns, and the

[1] It should perhaps be added that the demands of war have been an even more potent factor here.

73

countryside has been wastefully despoiled by unplanned siting of houses and factories and the pollution of rivers and the atmosphere. In towns, slum housing areas and derelict factory sites have been allowed to develop and remain as a problem for future generations.

Waste of labour and capital have been caused, as we have already seen, by the fluctuations of economic activity. This has been the result both of the trade cycle and of structural changes in industry. When industries located in particular areas face declining markets, the result may often be a concentration of derelict capital and unemployed men, and a waste of the 'social capital' invested in houses and public services. Similarly, in an area where industry is expanding there is an influx of capital and labour, and new houses and factories and public services have to be provided.

All these various forms of waste are symptoms of the conflict which may arise between private advantage and social advantage. Indeed, most of the other evils which we have been considering are aspects of the same thing. The individual business firm is concerned primarily with its own private advantage, with securing the best margin between the revenue it receives itself and the cost it incurs directly. Costs which fall on the community as a whole, such as pollution of the atmosphere by smoke, or loss of amenity, through the substitution of an ugly town for a pleasant countryside, or increased congestion of traffic, or the sacrifice of the rights of future generations to share in the fruits of the fertility of the ground, do not enter into its calculations. In other cases there may be advantages which are enjoyed by the community which are not reflected in the return actually received by those responsible for supplying the service concerned. For example, when a railway system is providing an essential public service, the loss to the community if it should have to close down would be far greater, probably, than the profits which the undertaking itself would forgo. Another example would be that of a business man exploiting a new invention, out of which he himself might make very little, but which might turn out to be of inestimable benefit to the community.

There is thus no guarantee that the pursuit of individual advantage by producers, even under the effective regulation of competition, will in fact coincide with the securing of the maximum advantage by the community. Often there is need for the State, as representing the interests of the community, to step in and redress the balance. The difficulty, however, is to find a criterion by which to assess the public advantage. One is dealing most of the time with values which cannot be measured, and the decision in what direction the public advantage lies must inevitably become a political one.

F. The working of the regulator of competition is hampered by the growth of monopoly, which is often inevitable for technical reasons.

In spite of all these defects and dangers and limitations, free enterprise retains its advantage in the provisions of scope for initiative and flexibility. The making of profits and avoidance of losses also remains the best available criterion of the economical use of resources. At the same time the regulating factor of competition, which is in theory relied upon to secure that profitability and economy coincide, is not so reliable in practice.

Although in many fields the average size of the productive unit is still small, there has undoubtedly been a trend towards an increase in size, though this is much more marked in some industries than in others. This arises from the exploitation of the internal economies of large-scale production. An increase in the size of the productive unit often makes possible a reduction in costs per unit of output, through the use of more efficient plant and machinery with a larger capacity, through more efficient organization and greater specialization both in the actual

75

manufacturing process and in administration. The extent to which these economies can be exploited varies according to the nature of the product and its market. In some cases, as where the product is highly specialized and very diverse, the limited size of the market or the need for close supervision to secure high quality may limit the scale of production. In other cases, external economies arising from the specialization of different firms on different related products or processes within a single geographical area may outweigh the possible internal economies and thus there may be no advantages in an increase of size. In other cases, however, such as the iron and steel, cement and chemical industries, or electricity supply, the large-scale integrated plant has outstanding advantages.

Although there is thus a great difference of degree, the general tendency is nevertheless towards an increase of scale, and this applies to the size of firms even more than to the size of plants. This means both that the number of firms engaged in a particular branch of production is usually smaller than it was, and also that there are often one or two big ones which may well control enough of the market to have some influence on the level of prices. Thus even where the number of firms in an industry is still large, it is common to find a kind of price leadership exercised by the bigger ones. By their own actions they largely fix the price policy and product qualities which will prevail in the industry, and the smaller firms have to follow their lead. Along with this goes an increasing tendency towards the formation of trade associations which are often in a position to fix prices, and sometimes output also, for most of the firms in the industry. The growth in influence of these associations was aided by the increase in the size and reduction in the number of firms. In Britain it was further encouraged by the conditions of the inter-war period, with contracting export markets instead of the expansion of the nineteenth century, and with the growing importance of the more easily controlled home market. Their position was still further strengthened by wartime controls, for the Government found it necessary to work through them in controlling production.

Thus, over wide sectors of the economy, the regulating force of competition has become increasingly less effective. Although complete control of a market by one or two producers is uncommon, the general pattern has come to be more than of what is called monopolistic competition than anything resembling the perfect competition of the text books. In other words, the number of producers is often small enough for most of them to be able to exercise some degree of control over their markets. Under these circumstances, the tendency is to avoid price competition, either by explicit agreement, or through a tacit understanding of the disadvantageous effect of the price war that would follow attempts to cut prices. There may still be keen competition to sell goods at the accepted prices, but it tends to take the form of varying the quality of the product, of the branding of goods, of advertising and the offering of services along with the goods. In many cases this position is strengthened by resale price maintenance agreements, which prevent wholesalers and retailers from selling branded goods below the prices fixed by the manufacturers.[1] In many cases also these tendencies have been further encouraged by the growth of protective tariffs and quotas, which limit the extent of competition of foreign goods in the home market, and thus make it easier for home producers to secure control of their markets.

The extent to which these tendencies apply is natually much greater in some sections of the economy than in others. Much agricultural production, for instance, is carried on under conditions not so unlike those of perfect competition, for in agriculture the relatively small-scale productive unit has an advantage, and

[1] The Lloyd Jacobs Committee published accounts of resale price maintenance through trade associations in the following trades: toilet and medicinal preparations, hairdressing and hairdressing articles, groceries, cigarettes and tobacco, chocolate and sugar confectionery, stationery, books, hardware, bicycles and motor-cycles, motor vehicles and accessories, electrical goods, electric lamps, radio valves, refrigerators and refrigeration equipment, and dental goods. *Report of the Committee on Resale Price Maintenance*, Cmd. 7696, 1949.

the staple products, such as wheat or cotton or milk or meat, tend to be relatively homogeneous and not adapted to differentiation by producers. In order to protect farmers from the insecurity which results from dependence on the fluctuations of world prices, there has, however, been an increasing tendency towards the introduction of protective measures with state support. Thus import markets come to be protected by tariffs and quotas, and farmers' incomes are guaranteed by price fixing and output regulation schemes, while products are coming increasingly to be graded and sold through centralized marketing agencies. In the industrial field, also, there are industries like cotton and woollens in which firms tend to be small and products to fall into standard grades not differentiated according to their producers. In the case of most goods manufactured for final consumption, however, the tendency has been for the manufacturers, by branding and advertising, to seek to differentiate their products from those of their competitors, and thus acquire a greater measure of control over them. In other industries, such as iron and steel, chemicals, the motor industry, and electrical engineering, the large firm has such a great technical advantage, either because of the nature of the process or because it can exploit mass production, that smaller firms cannot compete with it, except in certain specialized fields.

It is therefore true to say that in one form or another there is a tendency towards an increasing prevalence of monopoly. This weakens the factor on which reliance is placed, according to the theory of free enterprise, to secure the closest approximation to the most economical use of resources. It is only in the limiting case of perfect competition—i.e. when the number of buyers and sellers is so large and the product so homogeneous that no individual can exercise any control over market conditions by his own actions—that the maximizing of profits by the entrepreneur corresponds to the optimum use of resources. Competition is the 'invisible hand' which is relied upon to ensure that the entrepreneur, by maximizing his own advantage, also provides the optimum quantity and quality of each type of goods and services to the consumer and makes the optimum use of the factors of production in so doing. The greater the degree of monopoly, the more it becomes possible for the monopolists to exploit the consumer, consciously or unconsciously. In general, a producer with a certain degree of monopoly control over his market will make a greater profit by producing a smaller output and selling it at a higher price, and this may mean that it pays him better to produce at less than optimum capacity. Where a number of semi-monopolists are in competition, this is in general still true, and added costs are incurred by each in making sure of his share of the market. Thus the consumer may be offered goods of a more lavish quality and greater variety, with special packing and wide range of free services, as well as costly advertising, when he would have preferred a less elaborate but cheaper article.

Perfect competition is, of course, an abstraction rather than an actuality. Almost all producers, however small, have some degree of control over their markets, even if it is only through the goodwill of their regular customers. In the days when productive units were numerous and relatively small-scale, however, it was not unrealistic to regard something approaching it as being the norm, to which monopoly was an isolated exception. It was then reasonable to assume that the free pursuit of enlightened self-interest by all, consumers and producers alike, regulated by the operation of the price mechanism in fully competitive markets for factors and for products, could be relied upon to ensure the most economical use of resources for the greatest satisfaction of wants. The weakening of the regulating force of competition has been part of the price which has had to be paid for the increase of productivity, for the improvement of productive efficiency has come about through the exploitation of the economies of large scale. The gain in efficiency has been undoubtedly great, and modern methods of large-scale production have made many of the conveniences and luxuries of life available at a price within the reach of the ordinary consumer. The price has been the weakening of the sanction on which the consumers relied for the protection of their interests.

The rise of monopoly and semi-monopoly has been another factor leading to the intervention of the State in economic affairs. Such intervention has taken two main forms. In some cases, the attempt has been made through the machinery of the law to prevent the growth of monopolistic practices and to compel the continuance of competition. This has been done with more vigour in the United States than in Britain. The Anti-Trust Laws are designed both to prevent where possible the merging of firms into groups controlling whole industries, and also to prevent the operation of agreements and practices between firms which are regarded as being in restraint of trade. The Acts have been enforced with some success, but it has been an uphill battle. It is not easy to force business undertakings to compete fully when the conditions under which they operate and their own immediate interests all favour a policy of limiting competition by combination or agreement. In Britain, the recently established Monopolies Commission is intended to work on the same principles, and legislation has recently been suggested against resale prices maintenance. In other cases, where for technical or administrative reasons a monopoly is essential for efficiency, as in public utility services like gas, electricity and railways, or sometimes in basic industries like coal and steel, a different policy is adopted. The aim is then to bring the monopoly under public control, so as to provide by political means the guarantees of efficiency which competition cannot provide. Thus public utilities are subjected to regulation of charges, dividends and quality of service, and more recently have been brought increasingly under public ownership also. The desire to control monopoly is also one of the motives for the nationalization of basic industries. The public ownership and regulation of monopolies, however, raises further problems, both political and economic, which we shall have to consider later.

In view of these defects in the working of free enterprise, it was not surprising that the community should gradually find itself compelled to intervene more and more in the economic sphere, by means of the political organs of the State. It is with the forms that this intervention has taken, and the problems which it in turn raises, that we must next concern ourselves.

CHAPTER SIX

THE NATURE OF
PLANNING

*1. Planning—conscious direction of economic activities—is to
be found along with free enterprise in all societies.*

The term 'Planning' has come into popular use in recent years
to indicate an alternative to free enterprise. To the apparent
waste and incoherence of the operation of free enterprise, it is
attractive to oppose the alternative of planned economy, in which
we decide what we want and set out to achieve it. In practice,
however, the antithesis is not so sharply defined.

As a word, 'Planning' is itself ambiguous, for in one sense
planning is characteristic of all purposeful activity, whether
economic or otherwise. The decisions and actions of those who
direct business undertakings under free enterprise are planned,
in the sense that they decide in advance the quantity and quality
of output, its method of production, and the price at which it
is to be sold (in so far as they can control their own market),
on the basis of their estimates of cost and sale trends. The same
also applies to the choices and decisions of consumers. The essential characteristic of what we call planning, as opposed to free
enterprise, lies not in the making of a purposeful use of resources,
but in the seeking of a definite purpose for the economy as a
whole. The essence of 'planning', in the sense in which we
have come to use the word, is the formulation of definite and
conscious aims towards which the whole economy is to be
directed and the adoption of deliberate measures of economic
policy designed to secure their fulfilment. In this sense, it can

be regarded as an antithesis of free enterprise, since the essence of the later system is that the general welfare of the community is held to emerge automatically from the interaction of the choices of individual producers and consumers, motivated mainly by their own conception of their own best interests. It is in this sense that we shall use the term.

In practice, however, planning and free enterprise are by no means mutually exclusive. There are some epochs in the history of society when the emphasis tended to be placed more strongly on the one than on the other. For instance, in medieval times and in the mercantilist era of the sixteenth and seventeenth centuries, the stress tended to be laid on the regulation of the economy for the common good, whereas in the early days of the Industrial Revolution the emphasis swung over in the direction of *laissez-faire*. Over the last hundred years it has tended to swing back again towards planning. This trend has been carried to its fullest extent in the Soviet Union and its satellites, but in the west also the defects of unrestricted free enterprise have led to a considerable reaction away from it.

At the same time, however strongly the stress may be laid in the one direction or the other, the economic system tends in practice to be something of a blend of both principles. The regulated and ordered economy of the mercantilists remained always more an ideal than an actual achievement, for, while the Government was trying to regulate, individual enterprise was expanding at such a rate that it could not easily be kept within prescribed bounds. In the same way, even at the height of *laissez-faire*, the Government had certain inescapable economic functions, especially in the fields of taxation, monetary policy and the enforcement of contracts. Moreover, the abuses of the unregulated working of the system soon compelled interference. Factory Acts were found to be necessary to prevent intolerable abuses in working conditions, and Public Health Acts to deal with the sanitary evils of the growing towns. Once interference began, the scope of the government action came to be gradually extended, as we shall see in the next section.

Moreover, even the totalitarian planned economies of the present day have not been able to dispense altogether with free enterprise. The state productive organizations in each industry have to be left some freedom, within the general plan, to adapt their output and sales to changes in the market for their products and in the supply of their factors of production. The collective farms are allowed to sell some of their produce direct to the public. Small-scale private enterprise, such as that of individual traders selling from market stalls, or individual peasants marketing their crops, cannot be eliminated altogether. Consumers remain free to buy what they want, within the limits of what is made available, and within limits also workers must be given some freedom to change their jobs.

It would appear, then, that there is a part in the economy both for individual action, following in the main the individual's own estimates of what are his best interests, and for collective action designed to secure certain pre-conceived social aims. In fact, both of these represent essential elements in the social order, and neither of them is complete or adequate without the other. No collective organ, however wise and however representative, can make a valid claim to be able so to order the economic affairs of men as to leave no scope for the independent vision and ability of the individual who wants to strike out for himself. And equally no society, however far-seeing and altruistic its members, can afford to leave its economic well-being entirely to the free action of individuals, without some responsibility having to be undertaken through its political organs to ensure a general framework conducive to the common welfare. Individual enterprise and self-expression correspond to an essential and vital element in a healthy society, and no community can flourish which does not give adequate scope for them. Collective planning and regulation also correspond to an essential element in society, and should embody that wider vision and purpose in which the sense of fellowship and membership of the community find expression. Both of them will in practice be fallible and imperfect. Free enterprise will involve freedom for self-seeking and the exploitation of unequal opportunities by those individuals and groups which have the power to do so. Planning also involves the danger of a forcible ordering of society in the interests of one particular group or class, or of one particular point of view, which are mistaken for those of the whole community. Each is therefore an essential corrective of the other, and both of them need the corrective of a wider and higher loyalty which transcends all human organizations. For the Christian, both of them have their essential part as means through which God's purposes for society must find expression, but both need to be held under judgment in the light of the revelation of man's proneness to sin and need for redemption.

2. *The scope for conscious action by the Government in the economic field has been greatly extended in recent years to remedy the obvious defects of laissez-faire.*

The scope for conscious action by the Government designed to direct and influence the working of the economy has greatly increased in recent years. The reasons for this intervention and the main lines which it has taken have already come out in our examination of the free enterprise system, but in order to get a clear background for the discussion of the problems of planning, it will be as well to summarize them here.

A. Promotion of greater equality—mainly through progressive taxation and the social services.

Action by the State has been increasingly called for to redress the worst effects of inequality of income and opportunity, and the main method has been the progressive taxation of incomes and inherited property together with the provision of social ser-

85

vices free or below cost. This process has been inspired partly by the desire for social justice: the realization that, with the growing wealth of the community, it was both unjust and inefficient to allow social evils to persist which could be mitigated by appropriate action by the State. It has also been the effect of the extension of political power to the less well-off sections of the community through the introduction of universal suffrage. It had already begun in a small way before 1914, with free education, and the first Old Age Pension and National Insurance schemes. Its scope was greatly extended as a result of the first world war, which made the nation accustomed to high taxation and the extended responsibility of the State. Throughout the inter-war period, the social services were being improved and extended, in spite of setbacks at the time of the financial crisis of 1931. The second world war, which accustomed people to still higher taxation and a still greater extension of state responsibility, has carried the process still further. It was quickly followed by the introduction of Family Allowances, by the comprehensive National Insurance Scheme of 1948, and by the National Health Service.

The State has also taken steps to help the lower-paid workers to improve their bargaining position. In the early days, the trade unions fought for and won the right to organize for collective bargaining mainly by their own efforts, in face of the opposition of employers and the authorities alike. More recently, however, the Government has been active in encouraging the development of voluntary facilities for conciliation and arbitration, and has also established compulsory collective machinery, in the form of Trade Boards and Wages Councils, in those industries where voluntary organization is weak.[1] This

[1] The total number of workers covered by compulsory wage-fixing is given by A. Flanders (*Trade Unions*, London, 1952, p. 91) as about 4,500,000. The Ministry of Labour *Annual Report* for 1951 lists a total of 65 Wage Councils and Wage Boards (excluding those in agriculture). The members of the Councils are appointed by the Minister and include representatives of employers' associations and trade unions, and independent members. Their wage recommendations are given compulsory force by Orders made by the Minister.

has been another influence working towards a greater equality of incomes.

B. Meeting of needs not adequately met by private enterprise, especially in the fields of education, housing and public health.

One aspect of this process of redistribution through taxation and the social services has been the meeting by corporate action through the State of needs which it was felt to be socially desirable to meet, but which were not adequately provided for by private enterprise. Among the chief fields in which this has been done are those of education, housing and public health. Primary and secondary education is now available in Britain free for all, in a form which, though in many cases still inadequate, is intended to be that appropriate to the aptitudes of the children concerned. Assistance is also given on a considerable scale towards higher education. Housing is provided by the public authorities at rents which are highly subsidized, and the main reliance has been placed on such subsidized building to meet post-war housing needs. The State has now accepted the obligation to provide a health service in all its branches, to a large extent without direct charge to the recipient. In the case of these services, and others, it has been thought preferable to provide the actual service, either free or below cost price, at the expense of the taxpayers in general, rather than merely redistributing incomes and leaving the recipients free to spend them as they choose. In the case of education, the use of the services or an equivalent is even made compulsory up to the age of fifteen. It is felt to be socially desirable that these services should be available and made use of, and that, even if adequate income is available, people cannot be relied upon to demand them effectively enough to make it possible to leave their supply to free private enterprise. People might prefer to live in slums to save rent and to send their children to work instead of to school in order to have more money to spend on other things, but education and public health are regarded as too valuable for them to be left to do this.

> c. Discharge of responsibilities in the field of international relationships, such as the regulation of foreign trade and exchange.

The Government has some economic responsibilities which are inescapable, since they arise out of its primary functions of administration. Among these are those arising in the field of international relationships, and in particular the regulation of foreign trade and foreign exchanges.

In the days when the belief in free enterprise was at its height, it was widely held that in these fields also active state intervention should be kept to a minimum, and reliance should be placed on the automatic operation of Free Trade and the international Gold Standard. The effective working of these, however, depended largely on the fact of Britain's undoubted supremacy as the world's centre of manufacturing, commerce and finance. Free Trade suited Britain, for she could buy her foodstuffs and raw materials from the cheapest source and be sure of expanding markets for her exports of manufactured goods, but it never found so much favour in other countries which had to develop their manufactures in the face of British competition. The Gold Standard worked because London was the world's financial centre and sterling the main currency of world trade. It was the Bank of England which worked out by experience the rules for the 'automatic' working of the Gold Standard, whereby changes in the balance of payments were followed by inflows and outflows of gold, which had to be counteracted by appropriate measures to expand or contract internal credit. Because of Britain's dominant position in the world, the fact that the Bank of England kept to the rules meant that the whole system worked satisfactorily, for actions in London could be relied upon to produce the appropriate reactions elsewhere. Britain's position was already being challenged before 1914, and the dislocations of the war of 1914-18 brought the old system to an end. Although in the 1920's a precarious equilibrium was re-established, largely thanks to large-scale American lending, the depression of 1929-32 brought about a second collapse, which proved to be permanent. Governments found themselves bound to take active measures to protect their countries' economies against the effects of adverse balances of payments abroad and widespread unemployment at home. They were thus led to restrict and regulate imports by means of tariffs and quotas and import licences, and in many cases to control their foreign exchanges also. The advent of the second world war brought with it complete control both of foreign trade and foreign exchanges, and the dislocations of the post-war period have so far meant that the return to more liberal methods has been slow and partial.

> D. Acceptance of the responsibility for the mainten-
> ance of economic stability—holding the balance
> between unemployment and inflation.

There were other functions of government also which brought with them inescapable economic responsibilities. Of these, two of the most important were the impact of fiscal policy, of the level and distribution of taxation and government spending, on the economy, and the responsibility for the control of the monetary system. In both of these cases also, the nineteenth-century belief was in as much autonomy as possible. Government spending and hence taxation should be reduced to a minimum, while the regulation of money and credit should be left to the operation of an independent Central Bank, following the rules of the Gold Standard. In both cases, the factors which led to the adoption of a more positive policy by the Government were two-fold: the inflationary effects of large-scale government spending in wartime and the experience of heavy unemployment in the inter-war period. These were reflected in a change of emphasis on the part of economic theorists. Under the influence of the inter-war experience of severe unemployment, Keynes and his followers[1] came to lay stress on the importance of maintaining an effective demand for labour in order to secure full employment. Experience of post-war inflation has similarly led to emphasis on the need for action to restrain a demand which exceeds the available resources. When the level of government spending is so high that it induces inflation, as in wartime, then the Government must adopt anti-inflationary measures, increasing taxation, cutting down spending on scarce civilian goods through rationing and controls on prices and production, encouraging saving, and discouraging credit creation for non-essential purposes. Again, when it became obvious that the economic system, left to itself, could not be relied upon to produce a level of investment and effective demand adequate to ensure full employment, it came gradually to be accepted that the Government had the duty of redressing the balance by increasing its own spending and by encouraging consumption and investment by reducing taxation and stimulating credit expansion.

It is now generally agreed, therefore, that the Government has the responsibility of using the instruments of fiscal and monetary policy to hold the balance between unemployment and inflation. In recent years, there has been plenty of scope for anti-inflationary policies, and they have been pursued in Britain with some degree of success. The effectiveness of policies designed to avert the onset of a depression has not yet been properly tested. The depression of 1929-32 broke upon the world before such policies had been formulated, and although in several countries, notably the United States, attempts were made to stimulate recovery by extensive government spending, in most cases they were not carried far enough. The greatest degree of success was probably achieved in Germany and Japan, but here the domi-

---

[1] Similar lines of thought were being developed independently in other countries—e.g. by the Swedish economists and by Schumpeter in Germany and the United States.

nant motive towards government spending was the building up of military power, and full employment was achieved to some extent incidentally.

E. Experience of a fully controlled economy in time of war.

It will already have become clear that one of the greatest influences towards the extension of the scope of the economic responsibility of governments has been the experience of large-scale war. The scale and speed of mobilization of national resources required for modern warfare are far too great to be left to the free play of private enterprise regulated by the price system; such freedom would both be ineffective and cause severe hardship. War essentially involves the diversion of a very large part of the country's resources towards the production of goods and services which will not enter into final consumption. It thus brings about a great increase of money incomes, through full employment, but a reduction in the supply of consumption goods; hence it tends to produce highly inflationary conditions. The Government finds itself bound to interfere directly, both to secure the necessary diversion of resources, and to restrain the inflationary effects. Thus it comes to exercise an increasingly complete control over the economy. Production of war weapons, materials and supplies is carried out directly on government order, and a large part of the country's manpower is also employed directly by them, in the Forces and elsewhere. Labour must be directed to secure that the needs of the Armed Forces, war production, basic services and essential civilian production are met. The supply of materials must be controlled, and increasingly it becomes necessary to exercise direct control over production. Scarce consumer goods must be rationed to prevent hardship, and prices must be controlled and excess purchasing power must be mopped up through taxation and war savings. There must be strict control over foreign trade and foreign exchange to ensure the best use of scarce supplies, and of shipping and internal transport to ensure that essential needs can be met.[1]

All this was discovered slowly and painfully in the first world war. The second war began with the acceptance of the need for fairly comprehensive control, but experience showed that this had to be carried still further in the exacting circumstances of 1940-44. It is natural that the success of such wartime experience of a planned economy, directed though it was towards limited and well-defined objectives, and helped by national acceptance in a time of urgent danger, should have had a powerful effect towards creating a climate of opinion favourable to the adoption of planning in the much more complex circumstances of peacetime. This is the more true in that there was a keen sense of the defects of the unplanned economy, as they had been experienced in the depression years of the 1930's.

3. *Planning can take different forms according to scope and method.*

The general concept of 'Planning', or the 'Planned Economy', covers forms of organization which can vary considerably both in the extent to which it is attempted to control the operation of the economy and in the methods which are used. A number of distinctions can usefully be made as a means of clarifying the various forms of planning. In the first place we can classify according to the degree of control which is aimed at—e.g. whether it is desired to lay down in detail what form the economy shall take and how it shall attain it, or whether the intention is rather to provide a framework of general direction within which the economy can be left to function freely. Secondly, there is the question of the extent to which public

[1] For an account of wartime economic planning in Britain, see W. K. Hancock and M. W. Gowing: *The British War Economy*, London, 1949—one of the volumes of the official history of the second world war.

ownership of the means of production is relied upon, as opposed
to influencing or directing the operations of privately owned
concerns. Thirdly, there is the question of method, how far it is
that of direction, the giving of orders or prohibitions to those
who control production, and how far that of inducement, the
influencing of market conditions through taxation and government spending and so on.

A. The degree of Planning—a totally planned economy,
or a general framework for free enterprise?

The first distinction can be roughly described as that between
the aim of Total Planning and that of the Planned Framework,
or Framework Planning. It is a distinction of aim and degree
rather than of actual achievement, since it is doubtful whether a
totally planned economy is in fact ever achieved. Some degree
of autonomy must be left to the productive units if they are
to be able to adapt themselves to unforeseen changes in demand
and supply conditions. Where the general aim, on the other
hand, is of the framework type, the actual degree of control
envisaged or attained may vary considerably. In aim, however,
the distinction is clear and valid. Where the aim is one of
total planning, the planning authority attempts to work out a
complete blueprint of how the economy is to develop over the
next so many years, and of the methods by which these developments are to be attained. In the plan is laid down what proportion of the country's resources are to be devoted to each type
of consumption and investment use and what is to be the target
output for each industrial group. Provision is made to control
the supply of capital, materials and labour to secure the working
out of the plans, and the prices at which the output is to be
sold are also laid down. There is similar planning of the
volume and nature of imports and exports. In other words the
attempt is being undertaken to make by conscious decision
all those choices concerning the use of resources which under
free enterprise are made by the interaction of the decisions

of independent producers and consumers, following market prices.

The most obvious examples of this type of planning are the Five Year Plans of the Soviet Union and the similar plans of the satellite countries. Making allowance for the retention of private ownership, the aims and methods of Nazi economic planning in Germany were very similar. In these cases total planning is the economic embodiment of totalitarian philosophies and the methods used by the planners are influenced accordingly. Although the underlying aims and the spirit in which it was applied were very different, the wartime economic planning of Britain and the other countries of the west inevitably came to assume this total form, as it became increasingly necessary to ensure the completest possible mobilization of the country's resources for war purposes.

In the framework type of planning, on the other hand, the aim is different. There is no attempt to lay down in detail what the production achievements of different industries shall be, and if 'targets' are suggested, they represent estimates for guidance rather than orders for compliance. Nor is there usually any attempt at detailed control of production or the use of materials and labour. Rather, certain general aims are laid down, which it is held to be desirable that the economy should achieve, and certain general lines along which it should operate in order to achieve them. For instance, it may be held to be necessary, because of the balance of payments, to bring about a certain degree of expansion of exports, or certain basic industries may be felt to need re-equipment or expansion, or a balance may have to be kept between unemployment and inflation. In order to stimulate and direct the economy towards the attainment of these aims, the Government may seek to control it in certain general ways. There may be, for instance, a system of licensing of imports and control of foreign exchange, or a supervision of investment projects, or the control of certain essential materials such as coal or steel. The Government will also seek to influence the market conditions under which private enterprise works by the operation of its own taxation and spending policy. Certain basic industries or services may be transferred to public ownership and so become susceptible to more direct influence. Within this general framework, however, reliance will be placed on free enterprise functioning in the normal way, the aim being not so much so supersede its functions as to guide and influence them in the desired direction.

Planning of this framework type, in very varying degrees, has become almost universal in those parts of the world where total planning is repudiated. Most governments now assume that they have the responsibility of pursuing a positive economic policy, rather than leaving economic welfare entirely to the automatic working of free enterprise. In some cases the means used go little beyond the accepted normal function of the State, such as fiscal and monetary policy designed to correct any abnormalities in the free economy. In other cases, and notably in Britain and Scandinavia and some of the other countries of western Europe, a more positive line has recently been attempted, partly because of the exigencies of the post-war situation and partly because of the political convictions of the governments concerned. The type of planning attempted in these countries, however, is undoubtedly of the framework pattern.

B. The extent of reliance on public ownership of the means of production.

The question of planning has become bound up with that of the public ownership of the means of production, although the two are in essence quite distinct. It is true that in those countries where planning is carried to the fullest extent, namely the Soviet Union and her allies, public ownership is an essential part of the social order, and it undoubtedly makes possible a fuller and more direct control by the planners over the directors of enterprises. Nevertheless the Nazis in Germany succeeded in exercising a very full and detailed control over the economy and in diverting its resources largely to the building up of military strength, without departing greatly from the principle of private ownership, though only by drastically restricting the powers of the owners over their businesses. Wartime economies in Britain and the United States have also demonstrated that, at a time of national emergency, it is possible to operate something approaching a totally planned economy with general acceptance and with the co-operation of the private owners of the means of production. Nor does public ownership in turn necessarily imply planning. The boards of the nationalized industries in Britain are intended to operate independently as commercial concerns, even though the Minister has the right to give them directions on matters of general policy. Professor Lerner[1] and others have described models for a form of economy in which public ownership would be combined with something like the operation of free enterprise by the directors of the public industrial concerns.

Nevertheless, in general, public ownership is thought of, and used, as a method of carrying out planning, since it does provide a method whereby the Government can exercise control over productive undertakings more directly and with less friction than it can where ownership is private. But its use in planning is not the only motive which has led to the introduction or advocacy of public ownership; a number of others can be distinguished. First, there is the problem of the control of monopoly, which arises in basic industries such as iron and steel, and in public utility services, where the economies of large-scale production rule out effective competition. Public ownership is therefore advocated as a means of securing more effective control in the public interest. Allied to this is the desire to promote greater efficiency in such industries and services by concentrating them into the hands of one or a few large bodies, which must be publicly owned because of their importance in

[1] Cf. A. P. Lerner: *The Economics of Control*, New York, 1946.

the economy. Then there is the general question of the social responsibility of industry, the fact that its controllers tend to be effectively responsible to no one, and the desire to overcome this by transferring control to bodies which would be responsible to the political organs of the community. Again, there is the desire of the workers in industry for a greater share of control over their condition of work and for that sense of status which is so often felt to be lacking under the present organization. There has also been the feeling on the part of the wage-earners that public ownership would secure them a fairer share of the proceeds of production.

Moreover, the adoption of public ownership as a means of planning also introduces problems of its own. There is the vexed question of the relationship between the controlling bodies of publicly owned industries and the Government. This causes little difficulty in principle if total planning is intended, for then the boards of the industrial undertakings are merely subordinate agencies of the central authorities. Under the framework type, however, it raises the problem of how to combine commercial freedom and initiative with effective responsibility to the community through its political organs. There are the inevitable dangers of bureaucracy which arise in organizations which are bound to be large-scale and complex. There is the problem of finding effective incentives to efficiency and enterprise. This arises under planning for privately owned undertakings also if the degree of control exercised by the planners is considerable, but it arises with special force for nationalized undertakings, for which the direct profit incentive is weakened and which can more easily pass on any losses to the consumers or the taxpayers. There is also the danger of a loss of economic efficiency through political influences, and the possible threat to political and social freedom which arises when the economic organization of society is subordinated to the political. The last dangers arise under anything approaching total planning of any kind, especially when it is inspired by a totalitarian philosophy, but possibly the

97   G

threat is more direct where the economic organizations concerned are publicly owned.

c. The method of Planning—direction or inducement?

Finally there is the distinction, emphasized by Professor Lewis,[1] between the two methods or techniques of planning, that of direction and that of inducement. Both of these can be used whether the productive units concerned are publicly or privately owned, and whether the general aim is total or framework planning, though it is true to say that total planning will rely mainly on direction, while framework planning will probably put more emphasis on inducement.

The method of direction, as the name implies, is that of telling the undertakings or others concerned what they may or may not do. In the more total forms of planning this will probably mean the giving of actual directions concerning the quality and quantity of goods to be produced, the uses to which they are to be put and the prices to be charged. It will probably also involve the direction of workers into the jobs where they are felt to be most needed and the laying down of appropriate wage rates. In our own wartime planning, it was found increasingly necessary to control actual production in order to ensure adequate control of prices and of the use of materials; thus we had the Utility scheme and a wide range of prohibitions of the manufacture of inessentials. In the framework type of planning the directions will tend to take the form of controls of imports, exports and foreign exchange, controls of scarce materials, the licensing of new capital issues and of building and similar less direct forms. There may also be some rationing of consumer goods and some control of prices and profits margins.

Such use of the method of direction is often essential when certain resources, such a basic foodstuffs or raw materials, or the foreign exchange with which to buy them, are scarce, and when the need for them is urgent. It then becomes necessary

[1] W. A. Lewis: *The Principles of Economic Planning*, London, 1949.

to allocate available supplies to the most essential uses. To rely on the adjustment of supply and demand through price changes might cause undue hardship and would be unduly slow, because resources are not always mobile enough to respond quickly to price movements. Under such circumstances, it may be felt to be essential to bring about an expansion of certain forms of production and to discourage others, even at the expense of some loss of economic efficiency, and the best way to do it quickly may be through 'controls'. On the other hand, the method of direction has serious disadvantages. It involves the setting up of a costly administrative apparatus, both in the Civil Service and in industry. It causes friction and frustration and hampers enterprise, and it is not flexible enough to meet sudden changes of conditions. Moreover, it is a short-term expedient, since is does nothing to overcome the shortages which are the root of the problem.

The method of inducement, on the other hand, relies not on telling industry and business what to do, but on inducing them to do it by influencing the supply and demand conditions under which they operate. The instruments used mostly arise out of the ordinary functions of government, the main ones being taxation, government spending and monetary policy. By varying indirect taxation, the Government can influence the relative prices of different types of goods and services, and hence the demand for them and supply of them. By varying direct taxation the level and distribution of spendable incomes and the profitability of business operations can be influenced even more directly. By varying the volume and direction of its own spending, the Government can also influence market conditions. Through its own investment programme and its control over those of the nationalized industries, it affects the general level of investment. Through its spending on public services it exercises a great effect on the level of incomes and of demand for different types of goods. By subsidies it can directly influence the prices of certain goods which it is desired to make available more cheaply. Through its control of the monetary and credit system, the general level of economic activity can be influenced. Thus the methods used by governments to combat inflation and unemployment come mainly under the head of inducement.

On the whole, the method of inducement operates more smoothly and is more flexible than that of direction, since it does not cut across the immediate interests of producers and consumers, but seeks rather to influence them so that they are led voluntarily to adopt the desired course. There is therefore less friction and less need for a costly apparatus of administration. Inducement alone, however, is not usually adequate to deal with acute shortages and urgent needs, since resources are not mobile enough to flow quickly in the desired directions under the stimulus of market conditions. For instance, it is unlikely that Britain could have met her acute balance of payments problems in the immediate post-war years by inducement alone. There had to be control of imports and foreign exchange to ensure that essential needs were met and dollars were economized. So long as supplies of coal, steel, timber, etc., were inadequate to meet essential needs, their use had to be controlled, by direct allocation, rather than by influencing the price mechanism. Similarly in the case of essential foodstuffs, reliance on allocation by price instead of rationing might have caused extreme hardship to the less well-off. In this case, the social need for basic foods at reasonable prices has led to the continuance of food subsidies, which are a form of inducement policy, but this policy would not have been workable without rationing, for it might have stimulated an increase of demand which could not have been met.

It will be seen, therefore, that the name 'economic planning' can be used to cover policies of very different types. The ideal may be that of total planning or of the planned framework, and which of these is adopted will depend largely on the ideological background of the community concerned. There may be considerable differences in the extent to which public ownership of the means of production is adopted, and in the reasons for its adoption. Finally, the extent to which reliance is placed upon the methods of direction and inducement will also vary, both according to the facts of the practical situations, and according to the ideals which inspire economic policy.

CHAPTER SEVEN

PLANNING AND EFFICIENCY

The trend towards planning, discussed in the last chapter, was the result of experience of the disadvantageous effects of too great reliance on the automatic operation of free enterprise. The narrow restriction of the sphere of responsibility of corporate action through the Government, itself a reaction from earlier experience of state inefficiency, in turn resulted in serious dangers and inefficiencies, both economic and social. There has thus been an increasing call for the conscious formulation of economic aims and control of economic policies by the Government, in order to redress these evils. In some countries this has been carried to the extent of total planning; in others the aim has merely been to lay down a framework within which free enterprise can be left to operate. Planning in its various forms has thus been the chief means used by those who wish to reform and improve the working of the economic system. In order, therefore, to understand how Christian responsibilities are to be fulfilled in the economic order, it will be necessary to attempt an appraisal of the extent to which an increased use of planning is likely to promote both economic efficiency and social justice.

1. Planning and Economic Efficiency.

In the first place, we must consider how far the extension of planning is likely to lead to greater economic efficiency. How far are the conscious formulation of aims and the deliberate drawing up of policy to carry them into effect likely to bring about a more economical use of productive resources? How far are they likely to enable a great degree of true satisfaction to be obtained from the flow of goods and services produced, the way in which it is distributed, and the way in which men and women have to work in order to enjoy it? How far can planning bring about the remedying of the various evils which result from unrestricted free enterprise, and how far is it likely to bring other evils in its train? This can most easily be discussed by considering the part which it can play in the solution of each of the main aspects of the economic problem.

A. The Problem of Demand.

In the direct solution of the problem of demand, planning has little to offer. Since men's natures are so various, and since each has his own individual gifts and talents to develop, and his own distinctive contribution to make to God's purposes, in general each man must be left free to decide for himself what goods and services he wants to consume, and in what proportions, relative to his means. Consumers' sovereignty must remain the ideal and the rule, and any general attempt of the collective organs of the community to dictate what its individual members shall consume is fraught with dangers. Certain modifications of this principle have come to be accepted, as we have seen. There are certain services which are socially necessary which can by their nature be most efficiently provided communally, such as law and order and defence. There are others which are regarded as socially desirable which would not be adequately used if demand for them was left to the free exercise of consumers' choice, such as education, housing and public health; these are provided free or at subsidized prices and sometimes their use is made compulsory. There are also certain other forms of consumption, such as those of drugs and alcoholic drinks and gambling, on which the community finds it desirable to place restrictions. Under certain circumstances also the Government, as representing the community, may find it necessary to restrict the general level of consumption. This has been done in Britain in recent years, for instance, to bring about an expansion of exports, to increase investment in industry and social services, and to carry out rearmament. The decision how far such interference with consumers' sovereignty should be carried is a political one and to be taken in the light of prevailing political estimates of the nature of the public welfare. But though it would generally be admitted that in many cases free choices by consumers must be limited in this way, yet ultimately consumers' sovereignty remains the most reliable criterion for the solution of the problem of demand.

One of the controversial questions of the present day is how far this principle of interference in the social interest with the free exercise of consumers' choice should be carried. In general principle, what we may call the Welfare State finds common acceptance, but there is a difference of opinion concerning how far it should go. It is an open question how far it is socially more desirable to provide people with a rather wider or narrower range of free or subsidized services, or to leave them with rather more or less income for free spending on what they choose.[1]

The impact of planning on demand, however, is not so much direct as indirect. It comes not so much in the way in which it is ultimately decided what goods and services shall be consumed, as in the decisions concerning what is to be produced and in what quantities and qualities and how income is to be distributed. In general, therefore, planning accepts consumers' sovereignty. Its justification, as against free enterprise, must be found in the range of goods and services which it helps to make available for the consumer to choose and in the extent to which it leads to a more equitable distribution of effective demand among consumers.

B. The Problem of Production.

It is the sphere of production that the impact of planning

[1] In an article in *The Times*, 19th October, 1951, it was estimated that the 'social' element in personal consumption, i.e. the element of services provided by the Government out of taxation, had risen from about 12 per cent of the total in 1938 to about 18 per cent in 1950, or from 2s. 5d. in the £ to 3s. 7d.

is perhaps most direct and most controversial, and it is therefore under this heading that it will be most convenient to deal with the chief problems of economic efficiency which it raises.

It has seemed to many to be unsatisfactory that reliance should be placed mainly on the profit motive in deciding what goods and services should be produced and how productive resources should be combined to produce them. It has been argued that the best use of resources from the point of view of the community is unlikely to result from the pursuit by all those engaged in production of their individual self-interests. We have already seen that competition cannot be relied upon to act as an 'invisible hand' and produce harmonious co-operation out of the clash and interaction of motives which are essentially self-seeking. We have also seen some of the disharmonies and dislocations which are in fact produced, the gross inequality of incomes and opportunities, the concentration of arbitrary power, the exaltation of acquisitiveness and the instability that shows itself in a succession of booms and slumps.

These criticisms have found theoretical expression in a number of different forms, among them the Marxist doctrine of the inherent contradictions of capitalism, showing itself in the conflict between the need of the capitalists for high profits and for low wages, and the resultant under-consumption on the part of the workers. It is natural, therefore, that the idea of replacing free enterprise by deliberate and rational planning on behalf of the community of the way in which production is to be organized, should be found to be attractive to many. In some cases the ideal advocated has approximated to that of total planning; in others, rather to that of the planned framework. We shall therefore consider each in turn.

(i) *Total Planning of Production—its dangers.*

That something approaching the total planning of production is feasible as a long-term policy has been shown by the experience of the Soviet Union over the past thirty years. It has been found possible by deliberate planned action to bring about a remarkable expansion of industry and a reorganization of the whole structure of the economy, in a country which was relatively backward industrially. The system has shown that it can be made to work for over thirty years and can stand the strain of a devastating war. The factors which have made this possible are due in part to the use of the method of total planning in itself, and in part to the peculiar natural, social and political characteristics of Russia. They can be summarized briefly as follows: First, an ability to concentrate resources on investment in the development of the basic industries and services, at the cost of sacrificing standards of consumption. Secondly, an ability to concentrate mainly on the internal market and to disregard to a large extent the markets for exports and the supply of imports. Thirdly, an ability to override, by political means where necessary, all obstacles to the mobility of labour, capital and other factors of production.

Yet in spite of these remarkable achievements, it remains true that the method of total planning suffers from limitations and dangers which are as severe of their kind as those of free enterprise. They can be summarized under the headings of inflexibility, lack of incentive to enterprise, administrative diseconomies, and the problem of social control.

Inflexibility. The first and most serious danger of total planning is that of inflexibility. The planners must attempt to lay down the volumes and the qualities of the different kinds of goods and services which are to be produced in the relevant period, how all the various factors are to be used to produce them, and how the product is to be used. To do this in detail for all the innumerable possible varieties of products would involve a degree of wisdom and foreknowledge which would transcend the limitations of mortal men, but even if they confine themselves to the main general categories and classes of goods and services, the task remains a formidable one. In order to do it, they must make certain assumptions about the future trend of supply and demand conditions, such as crop prospects, mineral resources, labour supply, population trends, trends in demand for exports and supply of imports, changes in habits and tastes, and internal and external political conditions. It is unlikely that these assumptions will prove to be correct, and, in the event of unforeseen changes in demand and supply conditions, the plan is unlikely to be flexible enough to take account of them. Failure on any scale at any one point is likely to throw all the rest out of gear. A failure or a glut of an important crop, a failure of the miners to produce enough coal, a worsening of the international situation, calling for rearmament, the loss of certain export markets or the development of others, the advent of new technical processes, the rise of new fashions; all these are liable to lead to some degree of breakdown.

It is unlikely, therefore, that the plan will in fact work out as hoped. The production targets laid down will not be attained, and the goods which are produced will not turn out to be those which are wanted. Difficulties of this sort have been the common experience in Russia and were to be found even in our own wartime planning with its much more clear-cut and limited objectives. Failures of the plan to work out as expected cause a great deal of waste of energy and resources. Too much is produced of one sort of goods and not enough of another. Production of urgently needed goods is held up because certain materials or components or certain types of labour are not available in adequate quantities. The consumers are likely to suffer from a severe limitation of the choice of goods available for them both in quantity and quality. To some extent, of course, these defects can be overcome by improvements of planning technique, but the number of variable factors to be taken account of is so great that planning is likely always to be something of a hit and miss affair. These difficulties are likely to be much greater in a country like Britain, whose economy is dependent on trade with the rest of the world, than in one like the Soviet Union, which is largely self-sufficient. They will also be greater where considerable emphasis is laid on satisfying the consumers and giving them as wide and free a choice as possible, than they are where it is possible for consumers' preferences to be largely ignored for the sake of what are felt to be the more immediate interests of investment.

The semi-automatic working of the free enterprise system gives it an undoubted advantage here. Changes in demand and supply conditions find expression in changes of prices of factors and products, and producers and consumers adjust themselves accordingly. It is true that this automatic adjustment through the market is far from perfect owing to the imperfect mobility of resources. Gluts and shortages are far from unknown under free enterprise and they cause waste of resources and hardship to producers and consumers. But on the whole the adjustment is far better than that of a totally planned system can be, and the waste and hardship consequently less. There is a case for the introduction of some measure of planning to smooth over the maladjustments caused by imperfect mobility of resources, but it is much more difficult to make out a case for the supersession of the price and market mechanism as the main method of regulation.

The undoubted achievements of economic planning in the Soviet Union, and other places where it has been tried in something approaching a total form, have not been attained without considerable waste through such miscalculations. They have only been made possible by a deliberate sacrifice of the immediate welfare of the consumer, in the interests of concentration on the production of capital goods and with the hope of an eventual state of abundance when the transition stage is completed. They have also involved a ruthless acceptance of waste in the human sphere, in the forcible overriding of objections on the part of consumers or producers, as shown by such measures as the collectivization of the peasants, the liquidation of the kulaks and the use of forced labour. It is thus by the ignoring of consumers' preferences and the ruthless cutting through of obstacles to mobility that the problem of inflexibility has been tackled, largely by fitting demand and supply conditions to the plan, where it is not possible to adjust the plan to conditions.

Weakening of incentives to initiative and enterprise. The second problem of total planning of production is that of finding satisfactory incentives to initiative and enterprise to replace the profit motive.

There is one sense in which the totally planned economy has an advantage in this respect, in that it can often call upon an idealistic loyalty to the cause, which transcends individual self-interest and can often evoke enthusiasm and devoted service for very little material return. The history of all totalitarian regimes provides ample evidence of this, and indeed this is one respect in which the totalitarian philosophies have stepped in to meet an ideological need which free enterprise, with its emphasis on self-interest, proved unable to satisfy.

Such ideological motives are more effective in solving the problem of incentives to individual effort, however, than they are in dealing with that of the efficiency of undertakings as a whole. In any case, it has been found necessary to use the incentive of increased earnings as well. This has been done very extensively in the Soviet Union, where payment by results is very generally used, and where differentials in wages and salaries are as wide as elsewhere. In terms of the Communist ideology, this is justified as being appropriate to the transition stage of 'Socialism', in which there is not yet an absolute abundance of goods, and in which, therefore, it is necessary to pay men according to the social value of their contributions, instead of according to their needs. In effect, this is a recognition of human limitations though the cause of them is seen in an imperfect organization of production, and the habits of mind which it produces, rather than where the Christian would see it, in something deeper and more inherent in unredeemed human nature. The Russians also make use extensively of other types of incentives, both positive, such as privileges in the form of rations, housing and holidays, and the conferring of social prestige on successful workers, and negative, such as the fear of the consequences of inefficiency.

The totally planned economy may, however, be at a disadvantage in that in each branch of production there is only one employer, or at most a few closely associated employers. The enterprising employee is dependent on the system of promotion and transfer which exist within the single organization: he cannot move freely among a number of rival concerns which compete for his services. This may tend to reduce his incentives, both to mobility and efficiency.

It is in ensuring the efficiency of the undertaking as a whole that the difficulty arises most keenly. Here again, zeal for the cause may inspire the directors and managers of enterprises to energy and devotion, but this motive is likely to be an undiscriminating one if it is divorced from the criterion of profitability. With the privately owned undertaking, the incentive of the need to earn a profit or avoid a loss is always active, even if it does not automatically lead to maximum efficiency. Even though the directors may be activated largely by other motives, such as the building up of a successful firm, or the desire to serve the public, yet they must make a profit or go out of business, and this is a continual spur towards efficiency. Even if the firm enjoys sheltered markets and meets little effective competition, so that it can normally pay its way with little difficulty, its shareholders still expect their dividends, and the management must preserve enough efficiency and enterprise to prevent losses and continue to pay them. If losses are made, they must be recouped fairly quickly, or the firm will not be able to carry on.

With the publicly owned concern, operating under a fully planned economy, it is probable that the criterion of profitability will have to be used as the only means of assessing the efficiency of the use of resources. The undertaking will probably be charged a price for the materials which it uses and the capital which it has to borrow, and it will have to meet its own wage bill and other expenses, and will be expected to break even. But profitability as a criterion of efficiency may be blurred, for the prices charged for materials and capital may be nominal ones, involving an element of concealed subsidy or taxation. Even if the criterion is in fact a sound one, it has not the same incentive force as it has under free enterprise, for if a state organization controlling a whole industry, or a large part of it, fails to cover its expenses, it will not thereby be forced out of business. The State will be obliged to allow it to pass on its losses, either through higher prices for its products or through various forms of subsidy.

The only alternative course open to the planners is to reorganize the undertaking concerned or to get rid of those held to be responsible for its inefficiency. In other words, the remedy for economic inefficiency has to be sought in the use of semi-political methods. In the total planning of Russia and the satellite countries, we find that such methods are in fact used. Managers and technicians come to be liable to severe penalties for inefficiency and ' economic sabotage ', and they come to work under conditions of insecurity and suspicion which in themselves tend to have a further disincentive effect on their activities.

In those cases were total planning as a long-term aim is combined with the retention of private ownership, as in Nazi Germany, the problem of incentives is likely to be even more acute. There is likely to be a direct conflict between the interests of the entrepreneurs, based on their estimates of profitability, and the demands of the planning authorities. Such a conflict could only be resolved by the introduction of some outside loyalty, which might be expected to transcend economic interests. The Nazis found such a motive in the ideal of national strength and preparation for war.

Administrative diseconomies of scale. The third problem of the fully planned economy is that of the diseconomies of large-scale administration which are inherent in it. The attempt to prescribe and control the form which production shall take, and the way in which productive resources shall be used, inevitably involves the existence of a large and complex administrative structure to ensure that the plans are carried out. Even if there is a good deal of devolution of authority to the productive organizations, there must still be considerable retention of central control. This will mean constant reference of policy questions from lower to higher organs for decision, and a constant need to obtain permission for the use of materials of various sorts or for the carrying out of certain forms of activity. The result will be a considerable absorption of time and energy and man-power, both in the productive undertakings and in the organs of control, and a good deal of friction and frustration. More-over, the need to consult higher authority at every stage tends to produce an attitude of caution and unwillingness to take risks, which is characteristic of what we call bureaucracy.

In a system of which the aim is total planning, it is likely also that the individual productive organizations will be large and complex. Whether public ownership becomes the rule or not, it is probable that there will be central organizations for each industry or group of industries or services. The individual plant or factory or farm is likely to be a sub-unit of a complex admini-strative hierarchy, through which all communications between it and the central planners must pass. The managerial and administrative diseconomies of scale are therefore likely to be reproduced within the structure of each part of the productive organization, as well as in the planning system as a whole. Such a result is in some degree the inescapable cost of a system of total planning, and must be set against any technical economies of scale which may be obtained from a larger size of productive units.

Managerial diseconomies of scale are by no means unknown under free enterprise, for they are inevitable as the size of the undertaking increases. In general, however, the size of under-takings will be smaller under free enterprise than under total planning, and in addition total planning superimposes all the administrative apparatus of the planning system on top of the actual production organization.

The problem of social control. The fourth main problem of total planning is that of social control.

Under total planning, the function of ensuring that production conforms to what are conceived to be the community's needs, which under free enterprise is left to competition, is deliberately taken over by the planners. The form which it is intended that the economic order should take and the ways in which it should develop are prescribed according to their conception of relative priorities. This means that the problem of social control becomes a political one, and the means through which economic responsibility must be exercised are political ones. It becomes largely a question of devising means whereby the planners, in formulating and enforcing their conception of what constitutes economic welfare, can be made responsible to the community as a whole, whose well-being is so dependent on their actions. Questions of economic efficiency are thus linked up with those of social and political freedom, and therefore the discussion of the issues involved is deferred to Part ii of the present chapter.

Thus the attempt to escape from the disadvantages of free enterprise and reliance of the profit motive by means of total planning of production opens the way to further dangers. Such a system is apt to be rigid and highly inflexible and hence extremely wasteful. It weakens the incentives to efficiency and enterprise and involves serious administrative diseconomies. It raises acute problems of social control through the concentration of economic power. It is therefore natural to look for a 'halfway house' and this we now proceed to do.

(ii) *Partial or Framework Planning of Production.*

Such a halfway house is generally sought along the lines of what we have called the planned framework, the attempt to formulate by conscious decision a general framework of economic policy within which free enterprise can be left to act. The hope is to combat the dangers of free enterprise, while retaining its virtues as far as possible, and also reap some of the fruits of planning without incurring its more serious dangers.

By such a policy the greatest threat of total planning to economic efficiency, that of inflexibility, can be greatly reduced, especially if it is possible to rely on inducement instead of direction as far as possible. No attempt would be made to prescribe in detail the volumes and forms and methods of production of different types of goods and services. This would be left to the free choices of the directors of independent undertakings, whether publicly or privately owned, producing for the market and following price movements. Planning would take the form rather of trying to influence the market conditions under which they operated. The method used would be largely the manipulation of government spending and taxation and monetary policy, together possibly with certain controls over investment and key materials. In spite of the problems which arise from the fact that rates of taxation are normally altered only by the annual Budget, this sort of control can be made much more flexible to meet changing circumstances than more detailed planning of actual production could be.

Similarly, the incentive of profit is not removed, since reliance is still on the following of market conditions. The aim of policy is to influence market conditions so that profitability coincides as far as possible with the desired lines of development of the economy. The divergence between maximum private advantage and maximum social advantage is tackled by attempting to divert private advantage into the direction of public advantage. Administrative diseconomies also are much smaller than they are under total planning, especially where inducement is the main weapon, since the expenditure of manpower which is required in the Civil Service and in business is much smaller, and the possibility of friction between the directors of enterprises and the public authorities is greatly reduced.

At the same time, it becomes possible to do something to tackle the worst evils produced by unrestrained free enterprise. The methods by which this is done, however, involve acting not so much directly in the field of production as in those of distribution and exchanged and of savings and investment. Thus the distribution of incomes, and the terms on which goods and services are made available, are affected by policies of progressive taxation and social services, and of indirect taxation and subsidies. The problem of instability is attacked by the use of monetary policy and by the variation of taxation and spending to combat unemployment and inflation. The effect on the field of production is an indirect one, through the effect of government fiscal and spending policy on the demand and supply conditions for different types of products and factors.

A more direct influence on production is exercised by attempts to control or limit monopoly. This may be done either by breaking up combines and suppressing monopolistic practices which are regarded as harmful, or by subjecting monopolies, where they are regarded as essential for technical efficiency, to public regulation or to public ownership. In this field planning has so far been less successful. In many cases an increasing degree of monopoly is the price which must be paid for the reduction of costs resulting from the greater technical efficiency of larger scale production. If undertakings are left in private ownership, it is difficult to compel competition, where the immediate interests of the producers lead them in the direction of open or tacit co-operation. If undertakings are transferred to public ownership, the problems of incentives to efficiency and of social control are at once raised, as British experience with the nationalized industries has shown. This problem of the increasing degree of monopolization is one of those in which the limitations of both free enterprise following the profit motive and of deliberate control by the public authorities are clearly shown.

c. The Problems of Exchange and Distribution.

There is more scope for the direct intervention of planning in the fields of distribution and exchange than there is in that of production, and its use there gives rise to fewer problems.

> (i) *The scope for altering the distribution of income between factor-owners at the source is limited.*

We have already seen that gross inequality in the distribution of command over goods and services is one of the most serious causes of economic injustice, and that inequality of gifts and opportunities, together with the self-regarding tendency in man, produces an almost inescapable tendency towards it. Even if a measure of planning replaces free enterprise in the inspiration and organization of production, it does not appear to be possible to dispense with inequality of reward to owners of factors. Even if private ownership of the means of production is abolished, so that payments for the use of capital are no longer made to private owners to induce them to release their resources from consumption for investment in production, the experience of the Soviet Union has shown that great inequality in the payments, in cash and kind and privilege, made to those who perform different types of labour is still necessary.

The self-regarding element must be accepted by the Christian and with it the need for a redemption that will divert man's self-centred energies into constructive channels. We must accept, therefore, that there will have to be some material incentive towards the encouragement of efficiency and enterprise and the acquiring of superior skill or training, and also some disincentives to idleness, incompetence and waste. There must also be incentives to mobility, to encourage factors to move to those uses where they are more urgently required and from those where they are less needed. The system of different rates of wages for labour and interest on different types of capital represents a price mechanism which has a flexibility which cannot be dispensed with. We cannot adequately replace it by any system of detailed regulation or direction of the use of different kinds of labour and capital. At the same time, we must remember that payments to the owners of factors are not only a price which is paid for the use of the factor concerned, but also an income on which individuals and families are dependent. Economic efficiency may demand a tendency towards inequality, but justice demands a counteracting tendency towards equality, based on the needs of men, and their dignity and value as all equally, though not identically, sons of God. Therefore if the market system contains a tendency towards gross inequality, as we have seen that it does, some intervention in the form of planning is necessary.

It appears, however, that the scope for bringing about a greater equality of incomes by acting directly on the conditions of earning is relatively limited. Something can be done along two lines. The first is to increase the bargaining power of the less skilled members of the community, so that they no longer feel the full effects of an excess of the supply of their services relative to the demand. This can be done by encouraging the spread of trade unions and by supplementing voluntary collective bargaining by compulsory wage-fixing in the less organized industries and trades, as has been done in Britain through the Trade Boards and Wages Councils. The second line of attack is to reduce the inequalities of opportunity which arise out of such circumstances as bad homes and inferior education, so that all those who have the ability to enter the more highly skilled and highly trained occupations have a chance to do so. That part of the scarcity value of such occupation which arises from the difficulty of entry into them would thus be reduced, and the differential between the earnings of those who practise them and others less skilled would come to be less. Both these processes have in fact been going on in the countries of the west in recent years, and in Britain they have advanced notably since

1939. When the effect of taxation and the social services is also taken into account, the result has been a marked levelling-up and levelling-down of the incomes actually available for spending. The differences between the spending power of the unskilled labourer, the skilled craftsman, the professional man, the land-owner and the business executive, though still considerable, are much less marked than they were even twenty years ago.[1]

But this sort of process cannot be carried very far, because earning powers are affected by differences of natural temperament and abilities and because of the need for incentives to effort and mobility. Already we hear complaints that the differentials enjoyed by the skilled craftsman over the semi-skilled or unskilled are no longer great enough to encourage boys to undertake the training necessary to acquire a skilled trade, and the same complaint is being made in some of the less well-paid professions, such as teaching and nursing. In part, of course, this points to the inadequacy of purely financial motives and the need to inspire and encourage other motives for undertaking more difficult, more interesting and more responsible work. It is doubtful, however, whether financial incentives can ever be dispensed with, and this is an inevitable limit to the levelling process.

(ii) *More can be done by redistribution through taxation and the social services, but this process has its limits too.*

It has been found easier to attack the problem of inequality, not at the source of the income, but through the fiscal power

[1] The *Economist* (January 21st, 1950, as amended on June 10th, 1950) estimates the real purchasing power of the national wage-bill (after deduction of direct taxation) as 20 per cent greater in 1948 than in 1938. The real value of the salary-bill was estimated to be about the same as in 1938, while that of the total of profits, interest and rent was estimated to have fallen by 15 per cent. These figures make no allowance, of course, for the changes in numbers in the three groups nor for wide variations of income changes with them, but they give some indication of the extent of the levelling-up process.

of the State. With the growth of the wealth of society, as we saw above, have come both a realization of the evils and dangers of gross inequality, and an increase in the political power of the less well-off. Hence we have the rise of the ideal of the Welfare State, in which it is accepted as part of the duty of the State to redress the balance, reducing the spending incomes of the better-off by progressive taxation of incomes and inheritances, and providing free or subsidized services designed to increase the security and the opportunities of the poorer sections of the community. This method of redistribution has the advantage that it can be applied by the direct action of the Government, without interference with the organization of production. Moreover, the psychological effect of taxation, even when levied in the form of P.A.Y.E., is less serious than that of a levelling of nominal money rates of earning.

Planning in the field of distribution has thus been carried a long way in those countries where this sort of policy has gone furthest. The pattern of what are called disposable incomes, that is the command over goods and services available to income receivers after consideration of taxation and social service benefits, differs markedly from that of nominal money incomes. The man with a nominal money income of £10,000-£20,000 a year for instance, was in 1951 only able to spend an average of thirty per cent of it as he pleased after deduction of income tax and surtax. The remainder of it was taken from him and used by the Government. Part went into provide services which benefited the whole community, and him as a member of it, but which he could not provide for himself, such as law and order, defence and public health. Part went to provide services which were available to him to use if he wanted, but which he need not use, and on which he might not choose to spend in that proportion if left to himself. Part was used to provide services directly for the benefit of those less well-off than himself, and of which he got the benefit only indirectly, through living in a healthier and more stable community. The average man with

£150-£250 a year, on the other hand, was left with nearly ninety-eight per cent of his income after payment of income tax and was able to enjoy a wide range of services which he could not possibly afford for himself and might not choose to spend on if he could, though, on the other hand, especially if he were a smoker or a drinker, he would pay relatively more heavily in indirect taxation.[1]

The experience of Britain over the past twelve years or so shows that it is possible without undue friction to carry this process to lengths which would have appeared incredible only a short time ago. This is due partly to the general prosperity of the country and the full employment of its resources, which have arisen largely from factors outside our control, such as the long continuance of post-war boom conditions and the urgent needs for exports and capital investment. Yet there are not wanting signs that it would be difficult to carry it much further. The level of taxation is high enough to begin to have disincentive effects on effort and enterprise, as well as accentuating the problem of tax evasion. With the extension of indirect taxation, such as purchase tax and the duties on tobacco and alcoholic drinks, redistribution of income has come to be very largely between those who consume taxed articles and those who do not rather than between different income groups. The high level of taxation is due, it is true, not only to spending on the social services, but also to a high level of spending on other things such as defence, administration and the service of the national debt, as well as of the need for a Budget surplus to check inflation. If defence spending at the present and contemplated level were not necessary, it might be possible to extend the social services and at the same time reduce taxation. There is also the problem of the effects of the social services themselves on economic efficiency. Social security ought to make for greater efficiency by improving health and reducing

[1] *Ninety-fourth Report of the Commissioners of Inland Revenue*, 1950-51, Cmd. 8436, Table 110.

anxiety concerning the consequences of sickness, unemployment and old age, but there is the possibility also that it may reduce the incentives to work hard, by reducing the fear of the sack and lessening the need to provide against emergencies to one-self or one's family. This danger is probably more acute at a time of full employment, and so is the further one that social security may act as a disincentive to mobility. If the extent and scope of the benefits were still further extended, the question whether the disincentive effects were likely to exceed the incentive ones would have to be considered.

Against these possible dangers must be set the undoubted fact that social security gives to a man and his family an assurance of minimum needs which is of the greatest value as an aid to the dignity and stability of family life, as well as a practical expression through communal action of a concern for the welfare of the neighbour which is essentially Christian in inspiration. But the fact that these doubts can be raised and must be seriously considered suggests that there are limits to this process of planned redistribution of income through the fiscal actions of the State. A point is reached at which the benefits of achieving a juster and more rational distribution, through the provision of social services, has to be balanced against the exercise of the responsibility which is laid upon all men to spend their own incomes in the way that seems best to them, in the fulfilment of their duty towards themselves, their families and the community.

(iii) Planning of the relative terms on which goods and services are exchanged.

Our consideration of the part to be played by planning in distribution covers the field of exchange also, since the one is the obverse of the other. The way in which command over goods and services is distributed is reflected in the terms on which different kinds of goods and services are exchanged against one another. If certain kinds of goods or services, such as educational facilities, or housing, or provision against misfortune, or medical service, or basic foodstuffs, are provided either free or at a price which is below cost, that will affect the demand both for them and their close substitutes and for other things on which the released purchasing power is spent. Similarly, demand is affected by taxation, which absorbs purchasing power whether it is direct or indirect. By means of a system of indirect taxes and subsidies, it is possible to produce a pattern of price relationships between certain types of goods which may differ considerably from that which would be produced by the forces of supply and demand acting by themselves. For instance, it may be felt to be socially desirable to discourage the consumption of certain luxuries, such as tobacco, alcoholic drinks and expensive clothing, and to encourage the consumption of basic foodstuffs like bread and meat or sugar or milk. Alternatively, the aim may be to discourage the consumption of certain imported goods in favour of those produced at home. All this can be done by altering the pattern of prices through fiscal action.

This policy also has its limitations, and involves the risk of discouraging the most economical use of resources. It is, of course, the classical Free Trade argument that Protection is wasteful. It involves consuming more costly home-produced products instead of cheaper imported ones and thus using more resources for a small return in satisfaction. It also reduces the effect of competition as a stimulus to efficiency. The same arguments can be used against subsidies with even greater force, for they stimulate a greater demand for the product concerned than would arise at an economic price, and thus a greater diversion of resources into producing it. Indeed, this fact is a cause of difficulty where subsidies are applied to goods which are scarce relative to potential demand. If rationing by price is prevented by the use of subsidies, in order to prevent hardship, the commodity itself must sometimes be rationed, because the demand cannot be fully met at the subsidized price. Subsidies also protect the inefficient producer, by securing for him a guaranteed return which is not passed on to the consumer, and they give the efficient producer a return greater than that at which he might be willing to sell. Indirect taxation, such as purchase tax, has the reverse effect of discouraging demand for the goods affected, and thus preventing the expansion of certain types of production which might take place at the economic price.

There are undoubtedly circumstances under which such interferences with the free working of the market system can be justified. Economic efficiency, in the sense of the extraction of the maximum volume of goods and services from the minimum use of the factors of production, is a means to an end, rather than an end itself. There are other aspects of social welfare which may be held to be worth achieving at the expense of some sacrifice of economic wealth. One of these aims is the stability which, in times of international economic disturbance, may be obtained by some degree of protection of home producers. Another is the development of new industries which cannot yet stand on their own feet in the face of foreign competition—the famous 'Infant Industry Argument'. Another is the discouragement of certain forms of consumption which are generally agreed to be socially undesirable in excess and the encouragement of other forms held to be socially desirable. Allied to this is the use of subsidies and indirect taxes at a time of rising prices, to draw off an inflationary excess of purchasing power through higher prices for non-essentials, while keeping down the price of certain essentials to discourage wage increases.

The limit to the use of such methods of planning exchange lies in the fact that they involve the modification of the price mechanism, so that it reflects not only the economic factors of cost and demand, but also the results of social valuations whose quantitative expression is necessarily arbitrary. By how much should the price of bread or milk be reduced below the level at which it would be fixed by market forces, and by how much ought the price of cigarettes to be raised above it? These can only be matters of political decision, and the way in which they are settled depends upon a calculation of social priorities and of the economic effects of various lines of action which must be carried out by the Government concerned. Since such interferences involve an arbitrary departure from the only objective criterion of the economical use of resources which we possess, it is probable that they should be the exception rather than the rule. This is true just as much for publicly owned undertakings as for private ones. The soundest general rule is that price should be based on calculations of cost and demand, and should not be increased by elements of indirect taxation, nor reduced by elements of subsidy. Departures from this rule should be exceptional and should only be made in cases where their social desirability is unquestioned.

D. The Problem of Saving and Investment.

(i) *The general desirability of planned control is accepted.*

The control of saving and investment is another field in which the desirability of a measure of planning has come to be generally accepted. As we saw earlier, experience has shown that the performance of these economic functions under free enterprise does not lead automatically to stable progress nor necessarily to the full use of resources, but rather to a succession of booms and slumps which cause a great deal of waste and hardship. The experience of the evils of large-scale unemployment in the 1930's led to general agreement that the securing of full employment and a more stable development of the economy were among the functions which the Government must undertake in the interests of general welfare.

Although it is accepted that some planning of saving and investment is necessary, there is room for much argument about how far the planning process should be carried. It is generally agreed that it must go further than the exercise of the inescapable governmental function of controlling the monetary system. Monetary policy, though it has its part to play, is not enough by itself; it must be combined with fiscal and budgetary policy. Taxation and government spending must be varied with the aim of incurring a deficit or running a surplus, according as the danger is of unemployment in inflation. The Government cannot rely upon inducing or discouraging the necessary saving or investment in the private sector of the economy; it must undertake to save or invest, as the case may be, to the extent that this is necessary to make good the deficiencies of private enterprise.

(ii) *Should planning supersede free enterprise here?*

When we go beyond this point the matter becomes much more controversial. Three main lines of approach can be distinguished. The first is that which conceives of the responsibility of the State as being that of regulating free enterprise, restraining its excesses and supplementing its deficiencies. The initiative in the development of the economic system would be left to the private savers and investors. The supply of savings would still come mainly from individuals and independent business firms, and the nature and direction of investment would still depend mainly on entrepreneurs' estimates of probable returns. The second line of approach is that which, while recognizing the part which free enterprise must play, and envisaging an economy which is still mainly private, nevertheless sees a more positive role for the Government and its planning authorities as essential. The initiative in deciding the lines on which the economy must develop and in inducing the developments, it is felt, must lie with the State, either through its own direct investment or more probably through controlling and influencing private investment. The third approach is that of total planners, who either reject private enterprise altogether, as being based on exploitation, or relegate it to a purely subordinate role and would place the whole responsibility for ensuring the necessary saving and investment on the organs of the State.

The choice that is made will depend to some extent on the purpose which is in view. If there is felt to be an urgent need for investment in certain directions, for instance in the re-equipping of certain basic industries or services, and if the resources available are unduly limited, owing to the pressure of other demands on the economy, it may be felt that a more positive policy on the part of the State is called for. The prospective return on such investments may not be large enough to call forth investment on the scale necessary, but the prospective social return, in the form of benefit to the community, may outweigh the likely private return to the investors. This is certainly true of coal-mining and railways in Britain to-day, and probably of iron and steel and electricity also, to name some examples. It also applies to social investment such as the provision of working-class houses, schools and hospitals. Unless some scale of priorities is drawn up by the State, and some measures either of direction or inducement are used to carry it into effect, there may be a danger that the resources will be drawn off into other uses such as the making of light consumer goods, or the building of offices and cinemas, in which the immediate return to the investors may be greater, but which are felt to be less urgently necessary at a time of heavy demand on limited resources.

This argument is carried still further by those concerned with the problems of undeveloped countries. There is little doubt that the rapid industrialization of poor countries which are mainly agricultural, and have little liquid wealth of their own, can only be carried out by a large measure of deliberate planning. Private enterprise on the scale necessary is lacking in such countries, and conditions are often unattractive to outside enterprise. This is still more true where a country decides to rely on its own resources, as the Soviet Union has done. The programme of industrialization carried out in that country, with its emphasis on the building up on a vast scale of the basic industries, such as coal, iron and steel and electric power, and on the mechanization of agriculture, could only have been undertaken by a regime which was willing and able to sacrifice everything to the carrying out of the Plan, and in fact it was only achieved at the expense of severe sacrifices in the field of consumption and of drastic measures to overcome immobility of labour.

Planning may therefore make possible a fuller development of the economy if this involves the undertaking of investment on a considerable scale in certain well-defined directions which, if left entirely to free enterprise, might never take place. Nevertheless, there are dangers in pushing this policy too far. The planners' estimate of the prospective benefits of the schemes they foster may be unsound, especially if circumstances change in ways which they had not foreseen, and if this occurs on any scale there may be considerable waste of resources. At the same time the placing of restrictions on private investment, if carried far, may result in discouraging or preventing developments which might have turned out to be of inestimable benefit. Once again, the test of the market return, inadequate and unreliable as it is, is the only objective measure which we have, and there are dangers in replacing it to too great an extent by the more subjective criteria of political policies. It is true that private investment decisions, based as they are on expectations of future return, are as likely as government decisions to be proved wrong. Yet, because private investment is less centralized, the losses resulting from mistaken decisions are likely to be less and mistakes in one direction are more likely to be outweighed by successful choices in another.

Planning, however, need not only be a substitute for free enterprise; it can be used to further it also. Particularly important in this respect is the case of the small firm, upon the enterprise of which the economy relies to a large extent for the exploitation of new ideas and new products. The small firm has often suffered in the past from difficulty in raising capital, since its own resources are limited and it has not easy access to the market for new issues of shares. There may thus be scope for state action in helping in the provision of new lines of development. In Britain this duty has been undertaken by the Finance Corporation for Industry, an organization sponsored in 1945 by a number of insurance and investment companies together with the Bank of England, with powers to make loans to approved undertakings which have difficulty in raising capital by normal means.

The argument concerning the limitations of planned investment applies with even greater force to the case of total planning. By the exercise of a complete control over investment, and the drawing up and carrying out of large-scale plans covering the whole economy, it is possible to carry into effect schemes of capital development on a scale and at a speed which would be impossible for private enterprise, especially in relatively undeveloped countries. But this can only be done by means of a single-minded and ruthless devotion which is prepared to sweep away all obstacles, and it involves an inevitably heavy cost in economic waste if the planners' calculations go wrong, and often in human suffering also.

Planning can do much to remedy the evils produced by unrestrained free enterprise, but experience up to the present suggests that it cannot replace it altogether without a grave danger of considerable loss of economic efficiency. The answer in this case, as in so many others, must be not so much 'either—or' as 'both'. Both are necessary if we are to have an economy which combines flexibility and the capacity to produce a steadily more-efficient exploitation of natural resources and human skill, with stability and respect for the interests of the community as well as of the individual, and which will provide for its members both opportunity and security.

2. Planning and Political Freedom.

Economic efficiency is not an end in itself, and a system which was very effective in the production and distribution of wealth might well give rise to other evils which more than offset this success. In particular, we must consider the effect of the use of the methods of planning on social and political freedom. It might well be that the gains in economic efficiency which a measure of planning could produce would only be achieved at the expense of an arbitrary concentration of political and social power into a few hands, which would so hamper and cramp the freedom of action of the bulk of the members of the community as seriously to hinder that development of personality through responsible co-operation which we believe to be in accordance with the purposes of God.

A. Planning involves a concentration of economic power into the hands of the political authorities.

The exercise of power is the essential element in the political problem, as the choice of uses of scarce resources is in the economic problem. Community life demands a certain degree of concentration of power into the hands of political authorities, and a certain degree of restriction on the actions of the individual members, in order to provide a framework of law and order within which a fuller development is possible. The essence of good government is to ensure that this power is exercised in such a way as to promote the fullest possible development of individual personalities within the wider community. The experience of what we call western democracy suggests that this is best obtained when those who exercise the power are made as far as possible responsible to those over whom it is exercised, and the machinery of parliamentary and cabinet government has been evolved in an endeavour to combine such responsibility with the authority necessary for effective and positive government action.

The gradual development of planning has involved a steady increase in the economic power of the State. The Government has come increasingly to conceive and enforce its own economic policies, in order to redress the inefficiencies and injustices produced by unrestricted free enterprise. This has meant that many decisions, which were formerly the result of interacting choices by large numbers of independent producers and consumers, are now arrived at through deliberate choices by the political authorities. For instance, the distribution of effective purchasing power is now largely influenced by the Government's policies concerning the level and nature of taxation and of spending on the social services, and the general level of employment and economic activity is also largely influenced by the Government's fiscal policy. Relative price levels are affected by policies concerning import duties, indirect taxation, subsidies and price control. The volume and form of investment are affected by controls over new capital issues, building and the use of scarce materials. The consumption of certain articles is affected by rationing and that of others may be influenced by controls over materials. Certain types of services are provided directly by the Government and paid for out of taxation, and their supply is a matter of political policy rather than of economic choice. Such an extension of the powers of the Government has become the accepted rule in the peace-time economy of countries where free enterprise still largely prevails. It is very much more marked in such countries in time of war, and even more marked in countries where total planning has become the aim.

The result of the undertaking of such economic functions by the Government has been a great increase in the power of the political organs of the State. The power of the Government over the members of the community becomes much greater, for good and for evil, when it includes widespread control over how they earn and spend their incomes, and over the nature and direction of the economic activities by which they get their livings. There is a concentration of power in the hands of the Government and a weakening of the alternative and independent sources of powers which, in the free enterprise economy, act as counteracting forces. The independent authority of the business and industrial undertakings has been reduced, largely, as we have seen, because it was felt to be irresponsible, and there has therefore been a tendency to subordinate their actions to the supervisory authority of the political organs of the State because these are regarded as being responsible to the community.

There has thus been an attempt to reduce an irresponsible, but diffused, economic power and replace it by a responsible, but more concentrated, power. This has been further encouraged by the trend towards concentration and large-scale enterprise in industry and business, which has tended to reduce the effectiveness of competition as a regulating device and as a protection of the community against exploitation. This process of replacement has not been carried very far in the countries of the west, where the economic organizations retain a great deal of effective independent power, and where the power of the political organs, though extended, is still felt to be responsibly exercised, both by reason of the functioning of parliamentary institutions, and because of the attitude and spirit both of those who exercise it and of the community in general. It does, however, raise important problems which must be considered, especially if there is any question of carrying the process of planning further and of using it as an alternative to free enterprise. In the first place, how far does the replacement of diffused economic power by concentrated power involve dangers which more than outweigh the fact that the concentrated power can be made responsible? For instance, if the whole of an important industry is concentrated into the hands of a nationalized corporation, that corporation may be made effectively responsible to a minister and through him to Parliament, but, on the other hand, all those who work in that industry will be dependent for their livelihood on a single employer, and the community will be dependent for the supply of that range of goods and services on a single productive organization. The same applies if detailed planning control is exercised over the industry by a single government organization even if the form of independent private ownership is retained, as in the Nazi system. There are obvious social dangers from the abuse of such concentrated power.

In the second place, can such concentrations of power be made really responsible? It is not easy to make the exercise of economic power responsible in any case, for by its nature the organization of production requires that decisions shall be taken quickly and authoritatively by a few people and their instructions carried out. The scope for anything like representative control by the mass of those engaged in the productive process is always likely to be limited. A good deal can probably be done by means of Joint Production Committees and other organs of joint consultation to ensure that those who work in the undertakings concerned come to understand more fully the decisions which have to be taken, and that their interests and opinions are consulted. Ultimately, however, the decision must be taken by the management and carried out by the subordinate ranks. Business managements must have effective authority, and this in turn makes it difficult to make them responsible to the political organs of the State. If they are to have commercial freedom to take their own decisions, they must be left a great deal of autonomy, as has been done with the nationalized corporations in Britain, and in this case it is difficult to devise means of making them really responsible.[1] If, on the other hand, the ideal of commercial autonomy is abandoned, and the aim is centralized planning by the organs of Government, then indeed the productive organizations will be effectively subordinated to the political organs of the State, and economic policy will become a branch of political policy, but in this case all the safeguards of the diffusion of power will have been sacrificed. The power of the executive organs of the State will have been so greatly extended that it will be difficult to prevent its arbitrary exercise,

[1] For a discussion of this question of the accountability of public corporations, see Acton Society Trust pamphlet No. 1 on nationalized industry: *Accountability to Parliament*, 1950.

whatever the formal safeguards in the way of parliamentary responsibility.

B. Are the dangers of totalitarianism inherent in an extended use of planning?

As we have seen, these problems do not arise acutely in the forms of framework planning which have been practised in the west in recent years, because the scope of independent free enterprise is still considerable and because institutional and ideological safeguards are strong. They would arise acutely, however, if planning were to be carried further and if the ideals of free enterprise were to be abandoned. Experiments in total planning have so far been undertaken by regimes professing totalitarian philosophies, such as Nazism and Communism, and totalitarian aims and methods have naturally prevailed in their economic activities also. This makes it all the more urgent to examine the question whether the dangers of totalitarianism are inherent in the extended use of planning.

It is clear that, in the Nazi and Communist systems, the totalitarian philosophy is the inspiration of economic planning and that the totalitarian methods are thus the fruits of the underlying philosophy rather than of the use of planning itself. Economic planning is only the economic expression of an underlying purpose, the building up of the strength of the German State and people for world domination in the one case and the building up of the strength of the regime which is to be the instrument to bring in the classless society in the other. Both these ideals were regarded as having a total claim on the obedience and loyalty of the people concerned, and their achievement was held to justify the use of any means, however ruthless, and the imposition of any sacrifices, however drastic. Thus the people could be called upon to accept the foregoing of present consumption in the interests of future strength, forced labour and forced loans, long hours of work at low pay, restrictions on freedom of movement and speech, and all the apparatus of propaganda and coercion could be used to induce this acceptance.

There is no inherent reason why the desire to replace free enterprise by an extended use of planning should spring from any such totalitarian inspiration. The ideals of the planners and those who inspire them may obviously be quite different. They may merely think of planning as a more efficient means of organizing the economic order for the general good. They may have the strongest belief in the value of individual freedom and no desire to enforce their views of what constitutes the good life on to others. There are, nevertheless, certain dangers.

In the first place, the planners must have a purpose. If they are going to set out to re-model the economic system along certain preconceived lines and to establish the machinery to make it work in the way they think it should, obviously they must have in mind certain views as to what these lines should be. It is likely, therefore, that they will try to form the economic system into the shape which they think it ought to take, to bring to the rest of the community the benefits of their ideas of what economic welfare consists of and how it should be promoted. Unless they are extraordinarily humble-minded, it is likely that they will overlook the fact that their ideas of economic welfare may not be shared by all their fellow-citizens, and that some of them may prefer their own ideas.

Secondly, the enforcement of planning involves the use of political means, the exercise of political power in the economic field. If the planning is to be at all thorough-going, it is likely that inducement will be thought to be inadequate, and coercion will be used. The method will tend to be that of direction and prohibition, backed by the threat of penalty. The exercise of this power will form part of the political apparatus of the State, and will thus be responsible to the popular will in the way provided by the constitution of the country concerned. If, however, the planners believe sincerely in the fulfilment of their plans, they will be tempted to secure their carrying out, irrespective of the degree of opposition which may prevail among certain sections of the community. The greater the extent of power exercised, the greater the likelihood of its abuse, and the greater the difficulty of making its exercise truly responsible. The planners may not be willing to face a reversal of their plans through a change of government, and may be tempted to take steps to preserve themselves in office indefinitely.

Thirdly, the exercise of power itself produces the taste for power. Even where the planners have had no totalitarian aims to begin with, once they have enjoyed power over all aspects of the national life there is a danger that they will be unwilling to relinquish it. They may convince themselves that it is essential for the public welfare that they should continue to hold power, and take steps to prevent their displacement by constitutional means. Moreover, in the exercise of power they will have made enemies, from whom they may fear reprisals, once they have relinquished their authority. In these ways the exercise of power, once it is allowed to become arbitrary and unlimited by constitutional checks, tends to be self-perpetuating.

There is thus a grave danger that an attempt to undertake anything approaching total planning, even if not inspired by totalitarian methods, will in itself lead to the generation of totalitarian aims and methods in those who practise it. This will certainly be the case unless there are strong counteracting forces making for the preservation of individual freedom and the exercise of democratic responsibility which are able to offset it. We now turn to consider the possibility of this.

c. Can these dangers be avoided?

Is it possible for a great extension of economic planning to be undertaken without these dangers of totalitarianism arising? Can the counteracting forces of democracy be made strong enought to offset them? Certain conditions are here suggested under which this might be possible.

(i) *Deliberate limitation of the scope of planning.*

In the first place, the dangers could only be avoided if there was a general recognition of them, both by the planners themselves and by all sections of the community, and a willingness to accept the greater degree of responsibility involved. A recognition of the dangers would in itself involve a limitation of the exercise of power and this would mean a limitation of the scope of the planning attempted. Thus the planners would probably have to accept that it would be impossible, without sacrifice of freedom and undue concentration of power, to undertake the deliberate centralized planning of all aspects of the economy. They would probably have to content themselves with laying down general lines of policy only and leaving subordinate bodies free to work out the details for themselves. They would probably have to confine the use of direction to the unavoidable minimum and make use of inducement as far as possible. They would have to try to keep their plan flexible, so that it could take account of the conflicting preferences and attitudes of various sections of the community, instead of overriding them.

(ii) *Devolution.*

This would probably mean that there would have to be a high degree of devolution. Decisions on detailed points would not have to be centralized at the highest level, but subordinate organizations right down to the individual plant, farm or shop would have to be given considerable authority to take their own decisions. As far as possible, these subordinate bodies would have to be given effective autonomy within the framework of general policy. Only by this means could there be an effective diffusal of responsibility, giving as many people as possible the chance of making real and significant choices in the exercise of their economic functions.

136

(iii) *Consultation.*

A corollary of devolution would be consultation. In the drawing up of the plans, the advice of all those concerned in their execution at all levels would have to be freely sought, and before the plans went into effect they would have to have some means of expressing their approval or otherwise. Once the plans were drawn up there would have to be further consultation at all levels over their carrying into effect. Only by such means as these can all those concerned be brought to feel that they have a real share in the plans and a real responsibility for their execution. The effectiveness of this method, as against the imposition of plans by authority from above, was fully borne out by wartime planning experience in Britain. As Sir Oliver Franks[1] and others have testified, it was the practice to carry out such consultation as widely as possible.

(iv) *Machinery for democratic responsibility.*

In view of the greatly extended powers which planning gives to the organs of the State, it is essential that appropriate machinery for democratic responsibility should be devised. The method of ministerial and cabinet responsibility to Parliament, and parliamentary and government responsibility to the electorate, adequate for the exercise of normal political powers, is not by itself a sufficient check on the exercise by the Government of widespread economic powers. Consideration must therefore be given to the relationship between the different organs of government to which the exercise of economic powers is entrusted. How far should responsibility for planning be carried directly by ministers who are members of the Government and responsible to Parliament, and how far by independent Commissions or Planning Boards composed of officials and experts? What should be the relationship of such commissions to

[1] Cf. Franks, Sir Oliver: *Central Planning and Control in War and Peace*, London, 1947.

the Ministers? What degree of independence of ministerial control should be enjoyed by the Boards responsible for the operation of nationalized industries? What powers should be given to local authorities and what degree of independence should they have in their exercise? New techniques must therefore be devised. To the forms of these little thought has so far been given. Among the lines of approach which might be found appropriate in various types of cases are such devices as consumers' consultative councils, independent tribunals with jurisdiction over prices and qualities of service, and some form of 'efficiency audit' carried out by standing commissions with power to examine the operations of the publicly owned undertakings with a view to checking, not so much on their financial profits as on their economic efficiency.[1] Within individual industries and industrial establishments there are possibilities in the further development of joint consultation between representatives of managements and trade unions. All these movements are, however, still in their infancy, and none of them is adequate to act as an effective check at present.

(v) *Encouragement of autonomous groups.*

One of the most important safeguards against the dangers of concentration of power is the fostering and encouraging of autonomous groups strong enough to act as counteracting influences. A healthy society must be a plural one, in which the individual members have an active loyalty, not only to the political organs of the State, nor to the economic organization by which they get their living, but to all sorts of other so-called 'voluntary'

---

[1] Consumers' consultative councils have been established in various forms in connection with the nationalized industries, to represent the interests of the consumers. In practice they do not appear to have been very effective. Tribunals and regulation commissions have been more common in the United States than in Britain, where they have been virtually confined to the field of transport. The Transport Tribunal has control over the charges of the British Transport Commission. Efficiency audits have been suggested, but so far no experiments have been made with them. They raise obvious problems of conflicting responsibility.

associations also. If the economic organization of society is to become more highly centralized, it is essential that there should be a vigorous and independent activity by other groups, such as political parties, trade unions and professional associations, cultural and recreational organizations, churches and so on. The Church in particular, as an organization transcending national boundaries, and claiming a loyalty independent of that claimed by the State, has an especial witness to make in this connection, and, to a greater extent than the other types of bodies mentioned, it has the independent spiritual resources with which to make it. There must be a recognition of the fact that all these so-called 'voluntary' associations have a validity of their own in their own sphere, and are not to be subordinated to the political organs, except in so far as this is essential to the fulfilment by the latter of their own proper function of the enforcement of good order. The independence of trade unions and professional associations is probably of particular importance, even though it makes more difficult the operation of a planned wages policy such as might be found necessary in a more fully planned economy. It acts as an essential counterbalance to the concentration of control over employment opportunities.

(vi) *Recognition of the limitations of the planners.*

None of these conditions is likely to be fulfilled unless the planners recognize their own limitations and the dangers to which they are prone, and unless the community is vigilant to see that they do not get a chance to forget them. Thus they must not think, nor be allowed to think, that their plan is likely to be anything but a very imperfect approximation to a more desirable economic order, and hence they must be ready to consult the views of others and make modifications in the light of experience. They must recognize, and the public must see that they recognize, the dangers which come from the exercise of arbitrary power, and thus see that provision is made for adequate safeguards and checks and for the healthy development of alternative sources of influence and opinion. In other words, if the dangers of totalitarianism are to be avoided, there must be an awareness of them and a deliberate striving to avoid them.

(vii) *Importance of ideological basis.*

In this connection, we are brought back to where we started, namely to the importance of the ideological basis of planning. The development of a totalitarian ideology is hardly to be avoided, under pressure of the concentration of power, unless there exists in the community a strong and effective anti-totalitarian ideology, and such an ideology, if it is to be effective, must be a positive one. Since Christianity, with its insistence on the fundamental worth of the individual in the sight of God, and of the importance of the community as the area in which love of God is to find expression in love of the neighbour, is the only force which is powerful enough and deep enough to provide a really effective answer to modern totalitarian philosophies, there is an especial responsibility laid upon Christians to work out in the light of their Faith a social philosophy adequate to the needs of their times. The active prevalence of the Christian Faith, and of social ideals which take their origin from it, is the best assurance that conditions such as those which have been described above would in fact arise, should a greater measure of economic planning be attempted.

D. Conclusions.

Our conclusion must be that the introduction of economic planning in a comprehensive form inevitably introduces a danger of a trend towards totalitarianism. It is possible that adequate safeguards might be devised against totalitarian trends, but the dangers are nevertheless real and when they are considered along with the acute economic difficulties to which total planning gives rise, as discussed in the first part of this chapter, our verdict on its use cannot be a very favourable one.

Any attempt to redress the defects of free enterprise by the way of total planning, then, is likely to defeat its own ends. To say this is not to condemn the use of planning altogether. We have already seen that a certain measure of planning, of the framework type, has come to be accepted as necessary to counteract the economic inefficiency and social evils to which unrestricted free enterprise gives rise. Such framework planning does, of course, involve an increase in the powers of the political organs of the State. This increase, however, should not be enough to involve any serious danger to freedom, provided there is alertness to the possible dangers on the part both of those who exercise these powers and of the community as a whole, provided steps are taken to ensure that the exercise of power is made responsible, and provided there is a healthy community life, with a vigorous growth of voluntary organizations and other independent sources of influence. It is obvious that the Christian Church and individual Christians have a vital part to play here. They must witness the fallibility of all human wisdom and justice, and hold the political and economic ideals and organizations of the community under constant judgment.

It is the function of Christians to be the leaven which will keep the community wholesome and prevent it going bad, and the light by which the community can see the way it ought to go. If they are to do this effectively, they must not only know the Faith which they profess and the Master whom they serve. They must also know what their Master will have them do in the particular situation in which they find themselves, and the implications of their Faith for the life of the time in which they live. It is the purpose of this book to provide some help towards the thinking out of the problems involved in the fulfilment of this responsibility. In the chapter which follows, we shall try to sum up what we have discovered concerning the nature of the economic order, and God's purposes for it, and we shall try to see what are the implications of this in terms of the life and witness of the Church and of individual Christians.

CHAPTER EIGHT

CHRISTIAN ECONOMIC
RESPONSIBILITY

1. The responsibility of understanding the nature of the economic order and its part in God's Purposes.

The first part of Christian economic responsibility is that of understanding. We cannot expect that our economic witness will be effective unless we are trying to understand the situation in which we have to make it, the nature of the economic order in which we are involved, and the part which it plays in God's purposes. Some people, by reason of their talents or opportunities, are in a more favourable position for doing this than others, and all are certainly not called to do it in the same way or in the same degree: there are differences of vocation in these matters as in others. An especial responsibility lies therefore on those whose gifts or whose calling in life puts them in a position where they need to give particular thought to the nature of the economic order, such as economists, business men, trade union leaders or administrators, each in their several fields. But since all of us are inescapably involved in the economic order, through which we get and spend our living, none of us can escape the responsibility altogether. By our economic acts, and the beliefs and attitudes of which they are the expression, we each of us have our influence on the working of the system as a whole.

This book has been written in the hope that it will be of some help in the approach to these problems, that it will provide a basis for the thinking and action of others. It will be well, therefore, to summarize and define the main trains of thought which have emerged from our discussion.

A. Economic activity is an essential part of human life and has a positive part in God's purposes.

Economic activity, as we all know, is an essential part of human life. It is the means by which we use human skills and natural resources to provide for our needs. Because these human skills and natural resources are given us by God, and because He intends us to satisfy our needs to His glory, economic activity is not to be regarded merely as an unfortunate necessity, which must be attended to if we are to be free to devote ourselves to 'higher' and more 'spiritual' things. It has a positive part in God's purposes: it is a means whereby He is to be glorified. We saw earlier some of the ways in which this is to be done: the thankful receiving and enjoyment of good gifts which God has given, the possibility of providing more adequately for the needs of all men, the sharing in God's creative work through the exercise of man's creative powers, co-operation with our neighbours in the meeting of our common needs. We saw that implicit in all these uses was the call to stewardship, and that this involved economy, the making of the wisest and most economical use of the resources which God has given us. The problem of the choice between alternative uses of resources is essential here, since human wants are infinite, and available means are limited. It is the ways in which these choices are made which form the subject matter of economics, and the two general principles which we found to underlie the ways in which economic problems have been tackled, to which we give the names of free enterprise and planning, are essentially two different approaches to the making of them.

B. We are dealing with an imperfect world, in which men's selfishness and idealism must both be recognized.

In considering the ways in which these choices are made and the results achieved by different ways of making them, we must

143

remember that we are dealing with a fallen world. Man is created in God's image, capable of rising to great heights of idealism both in vision and achievement, but he is also fallen. Selfishness is innate in him as well as idealism. Any realistic account of human activity must take account of this two-fold bent in man's nature. We must not be over-idealistic and neglect the self-regarding element in man, which is in many ways the strongest, otherwise we shall be guilty of Utopianism, the imagining of an ideal state of society which would need ideal men and women to make it work. On the other hand, we must not neglect the idealistic element in man, the fact that he is made to respond to his Creator's love, that he cannot live by bread alone and needs something to appeal to his higher nature as well as to his more selfish and material wants. A purely cynical view of man and society is as false as a Utopian one.

In economic terms this means that the self-regarding element in man, which corresponds to something essential in him, his need for self-expression, must be recognized and used. At the same time, its limitations must be recognized. We must recognize that, if the world's work is to be done, the incentives of self-interest (or those of family interest as an extension of them) must be used. We must accept that, men being what they are, they are likely to work harder for the hope of higher earnings, and that they will need incentives of this sort if they are to be persuaded to train for more responsible positions, or to move to jobs where they are more urgently needed. We must recognize that business men are more likely to develop new processes or products, or to open up new markets, if there is some prospect of higher profits as a reward. We must recognize also that those with a surplus of income over their immediate needs are more likely to make their savings available as capital to those who are willing to undertake investment, if they are likely to secure a share in the profits in the form of dividends. It is along these practical lines that the 'justification' for profits and for interest on capital must be sought.

To accept the necessity of self-interest in this way is not to overlook its limitations. It is clear that men need other incentives besides high wages and a good position if they are to give of their best in their work. Our Christian Faith also makes it clear to us that self-seeking is not the way to happiness, either for individuals or communities, but that only through self-forgetfulness can true satisfaction be found. Yet self-interest is not the purely negative and evil thing which this might suggest. What God calls us to is not the negation of self, so much as the fulfilment of self through self-giving. Thus there is a self-interest which has a valid part in God's purposes, in that it is His Will that all His children should make that full and personal contribution which it is in them to make. The individual has valid claims in his own right, and thus up to a point the pursuit of self-interest is the expression of powers which He has given and intends to be used. It is in this sense that the self-assertion of the individual can be a valuable and healthy protest against attempts of those who hold political or economic power to use it for the regimentation of their fellows. It is only by accepting self-interest, with both its value and its limitations, that we can point the way to self-fulfilment, in the economic sphere as in the theological.

Allied with the question of the incentives of profits and earnings is that of the criterion of profitability. There is no other objective criterion of the economical use of resources than the making of profit or the avoiding of loss. It is only by looking at whether or not a firm, or other economic organization, has covered its costs out of its revenue, that we can get any idea of whether it is making an economical use of labour and capital and land in order to provide goods and services to the community. This is true in spite of the obvious limitations arising from the imperfect mobility of resources and the imperfection of competition. Although it is possible for the inefficient firm to make a profit, if it is sheltered from competition, and although the making of maximum profit by the entrepreneur does not

K

coincide with the achievement of the greatest advantage to the community, yet once we depart from this criterion our judgments become largely arbitrary. If a nationalized undertaking, for instance, is allowed to make a loss on its annual working which is met by a subsidy from the Exchequer, then in effect it has been decided that a more socially fruitful use of resources is obtained by, for instance, keeping the price of the service concerned below cost price and producing more of it perhaps than would have been sold at a price which covered costs fully, than by insisting on the full covering of costs. But how is it to be decided what size of subsidy will give the most socially desirable results? The choice between a subsidy of £1,000,000 and £50,000,000 will have to be taken on political grounds. It is because this is so that the criterion of profitability is usually retained, even where the direct incentive of profit-seeking has been abandoned.

At the same time, the limits of the self-regarding motive must be recognized. The pursuit by all the members of the community of self-seeking as the dominant motive for their economic activities cannot be expected to lead to harmonious co-operation, for self-seeking leads to strife and discord, and it is only when self is transcended by a realization of the needs of others that harmony is possible. Therefore a healthy economic order needs other incentives besides those of self-interest. Moreover, self-seeking, powerful though it is in each of us, cannot ultimately satisfy men's needs, for God has made men for co-operation with Himself. There must be a recognition, therefore, of the fact that men need a loyalty which transcends self-interest and in the following of which the self can find fulfilment. There must be in the community some vision of a wider purpose than the mere satisfaction by each of his own needs, a loyalty which is capable of calling out that extra strength and devotion which men will give to a cause which they feel to be worthy. Therefore our economic order must use self-interest as far as it can be used to promote the general good, and not try deliberately to cut across it any more than is avoidable, but it must realize that it will only go so far and that a healthy society needs something more.

Such a wider vision and purpose is one of the most essential needs of our own society to-day. We have seen the limitations of the liberal view of society, the belief that, by leaving each man as free as possible to pursue his own advantage to the utmost of his ability, the way was opened to the greatest good of the community as a whole. Men can no longer believe that they are doing the best for the community merely by doing the best for themselves and their immediate dependants. With the recognition of the claims of the community comes the opposite danger of totalitarianism, the belief that the community has absolute claims in its own right, which transcend those of the individual members. This opens the door to tyranny, for it over-rides the legitimate claims of self-interest, as expressing the in-alienable rights and value of the individual personality. The need of our generation is to find an ideal of society which recog-nizes the full value and claims of the individual, but also recognizes that he can only find his fulfilment by free and voluntary co-operation in the wider community. Such a vision, we believe, can only be securely based on the Christian Faith.

It follows that, in the economic organization of society, as in the political, individualism and collectivism are both necessary and both limited. Just as individual freedom is necessary in the political sphere, so is free enterprise in the economic, because it gives expression to the energy and initiative and vision of individuals, free to follow out their own ideas and reap the benefit of them. It is necessary also as a protection of the rights of the individual against the pressure of the community towards conformity. Planning is necessary in the economic sphere, as is government action in the political, as expressing the vision of the community of a better and juster order to be obtained by deliberate action to restrain and counteract the results of indivi-dual freedom when they are felt to go against the general interest.

It is an essential protective against exploitation by individuals or groups of the inequalities of opportunity and power which arise out of men's unequal gifts, and their pursuit of self-interest. As far as we can see, the healthy economic order must find a place for both of them, for either of them carried to excess produces both economic inefficiency and social injustice.

c. The meaning of redemption in economic terms.

Christianity does not merely take a realistic view of the nature of man and society, recognizing the strength both of selfishness and idealism. It points to the cure as well as to the diagnosis, for it witnesses to the fact that God has intervened in this situation in Christ and offers redemption.

The economic and social order shares in the need for redemption, which is not something confined to personal relationships, but something which permeates all of mankind's activities. The offer of redemption in Christ applies to man's economic activities, to the way he gets a living as much as to any other part of his life, such as family or personal relationships or the duties of citizenship. Indeed, these various aspects of life cannot be separated, for the whole man is concerned in all of them. It is therefore the obligation of the Church, and of individual Christians as members of it, to witness to the meaning of economic redemption.

The clue to its meaning is probably to be found in a resolution of the tension between self-seeking and the service of others. Christian experience teaches us that true self-fulfilment is to be found, not in seeking one's own satisfaction as the central aim of life, but in self-surrender, the acceptance of God's Will as one's own in loving response to His love. Thus in the Christian life there is no ultimate conflict between serving of self and serving of others, for both find fulfilment in the service of God. In serving Him, we serve our own true ends, and also, for love of Him, we seek to serve our neighbour's truest ends. Because we are fallible and sinful, in spite of our knowledge of salvation, we are liable to constant failure in this, and the conflict often seems real enough to us. We are often tempted to seek our own immediate interests and to forget others, or to rationalize our own immediate interests and persuade ourselves that they are God's purposes. But at the deeper level of the fundamental aim and direction of our lives, the conflict can be resolved.

Of the practical consequences of this in terms of Christian witness in the economic order we shall be saying more in a later section. We may mention here one or two directions along which the Christian doctrine of redemption can throw new light on economic problems. In the first place, although the Christian, being human and fallible, will not be insensible to personal material incentives, for his family if not for himself, he will nevertheless try to make the main incentive by which his economic activity is inspired the service of God. This means that he will try to give of his best in his own work, making of it an offering to God; he will try to see his work, whatever it may be, in the light of God's purposes; and will try to act as a faithful steward of the talents and opportunities and material resources which God entrusts to him. In the second place, in his judgments upon the economic order as a whole, he will try to base his values upon God's purposes. He will think of men's work, not as an end in itself, nor as a means to his own gratification, but as a service rendered to God, as a means of creative satisfaction to the worker, as a means of co-operation and fellowship between neighbours, and as a means of enabling men to enjoy the good gifts which God intends them to enjoy. In the third place, since he tries to judge society by God's standards, he will have a keen sense of justice and will be alert to see and oppose all forms of injustice and exploitation, whatever their cause—whether, for instance, they are the results of free enterprise or of planning. In such ways as these, Christians are called to make their witness to God's salvation and to be the means by which it can become effective in the economic sphere. They will, of course, fail in all these respects, because of their own fallibility, but in God's service the aim is more important than the achievements, provided it is being sincerely and thoughtfully pursued to the best of our ability.

Thus the Christian doctrine of redemption in Christ can provide the inspiration for a social philosophy which makes both free enterprise and planning meaningful, and also acts as a check on their abuse. But if this is to be done, the implications of the Faith for the outward forms of political and economic and social organization, and for the aims which should inspire them, must be worked out in terms suitable for the particular needs of the age concerned. There is no single 'Christian' economic or political philosophy, for Christianity is for all ages and all societies; there are only economic and political philosophies which represent the attempts of Christians to witness to the eternal realities of the Faith in terms of changing social orders.

D. We must not identify any existing or prospective economic order with the Kingdom of God.

The warning given in the last section is an essential one. While Christians must seek to work out the implications of their Faith in terms of economic and social philosophy, yet at the same time they must beware of the temptation to identify any particular social or economic order with the Kingdom of God.

Since human beings are finite, limited in understanding and fallible in will, it follows that all forms of human organization, however lofty their ideals, are similarly imperfect and fallible. It is not possible, therefore, for the Kingdom of God to find complete expression in any form of human organization. This is partly because there will never be complete agreement, even among men of goodwill, concerning the form which the organization of society should take in order to conform to the will of God. We all know how strongly convinced and thoughtful Christians can disagree on political questions, and we must expect that this will always be the case. It is also because any existing form of social and economic organization is very largely the fruit of the conflict of sectional and class interests, even when these are not recognized as such by those who advocate them and put them forward. We are all of us influenced, more than we realize, by the ideas of our own time and the interests of our own class or nation. A comparison of the attitudes of the business community and trade union circles towards such questions as trade disputes and the introduction of new methods of working in industry will act as an illustration.

We must not yield to the temptation, therefore, to defend, say, free enterprise capitalism, or democratic socialism, or any other form of organization, as being in themselves 'Christian', whereas opposing systems are not. Nor must we be in too much hurry to condemn other systems such as Communism or Fascism as being 'un-Christian', just because they are opposed to the 'Christian' system under which we live, even though on fuller examination we may be compelled to find them incompatible with Christian belief. While we must be prepared to advocate those forms of organization which we feel to come nearest to God's Will, yet we must be ready to see their defects and limitations and to do justice to the good points of the forms which we oppose. Nor must we damn as 'un-Christian' those who disagree with us nor be surprised or hurt at the disagreement.

One grave result of the failure to avoid this danger is that Christianity comes to be thought of as identified with one particular, often transient, form of social order. For instance, if Christianity is felt to have a vested interest in the survival of the capitalist, free enterprise, economy, the result is that, if this form of economy proves to be unsuited to changing conditions, there is a danger that those who favour changes in the system to make it more in keeping with the new needs will come to reject Christianity as being bound up with capitalism. Whereas in fact the truths of Christianity are eternal and independent of changing social and economic orders.

2. *A criticism of some traditional economic concepts often associated with Christianity.*

We have now completed a general survey of the Christian approach to the economic problem and the part which the economic orders plays in God's purposes. Before going on to consider the practical aspects of Christian economic witness in more detail, it may be as well to say a few words about one or two concepts which have either played an important part in traditional Christian thought on economic matters or which often influence Christian thinking to-day. They are, the condemnation of usury and its relationship to profits and interest, the doctrine of the Just Price, the belief that an agricultural economy is more natural than an industrial one, and the belief that the world's troubles are due to an unsound monetary system.

A. Usury.

The condemnation of usury, inherited from the Old Testament, was a commonplace of Christian moral theology in medieval times and its influence was felt much later. It was usually justified on the grounds that money, being barren metal, could not 'breed', and that therefore a loan of money, unlike a partnership in a productive enterprise or the renting out of land, could not create any return to be paid to the borrower. Its moral justification, however, rose rather from the fact that in those days most productive enterprises required relatively little capital, which could usually be supplied by those directly engaged, and hence there was little need for borrowing. Under such circumstances, loans tended to be mainly for the purpose of financing consumption, usually in cases of either necessity or extravagance, and it was natural to think of such uses as essentially unproductive.

There are few respects in which there has been a greater change of practice in the last few centuries. With the great increase in the use of capital for the purposes of modern large-scale industry and trade, and with the rise of the joint-stock company as an easy means of mobilizing widely scattered savings for productive uses, the payment of interest and dividends on borrowed funds has become one of the mainstays of the economic system. There is still, however, a sense of unsettled moral issues underlying the practice, although it is so completely accepted. There is a certain uneasiness in the back of people's minds about regarding the payment of interest and dividends on share holdings as being on the same footing as the payment of wages and salaries for the services of labour. This is to be seen in the distinction which we make between 'earned' and 'unearned' income. It has been reinforced, especially in the minds of many of the industrial wage-earners, by the Marxist doctrine, which sees the payments to capital owners as exploitation, the diversion from the wage-earners of the 'surplus product' which they have created, and points to such disorders as the trade cycle as evidence of the fundamental contradictions of capitalism.

It is therefore necessary for us to try to get our ideas straight about the matter. In the first place, it seems clear that the old idea of 'barren money not breeding' involves a misconception. As can clearly be seen nowadays, when most money consists not of metal but of credit, of entries in bank ledgers, what is borrowed and lent is not so much 'money' as such, as command over resources, purchasing power. The lender forgoes a certain amount of command over resources and makes it available to the borrower. This purchasing power may be spent on consumption, in which case it yields no product other than a transfer of satisfaction from lender to borrower. If, however, it is used as capital, to provide for the building of factories and the installing of machines, the buying of materials and the paying of wages, then, together with the labour and natural resources used along with it, it certainly does take part in the production of a product. There is no doubt that the use of stored-up wealth in the form of capital makes possible the creation of a larger product for a given expenditure of labour and natural resources, for most of the progress of modern industry consists of just such an increasing use of capital.

In the earlier days of economic theory, there was a good deal of discussion concerning how far the product could be held to be that of the labour, the capital, or the natural resources, but experience has shown that such discussion is largely sterile. The fact remains that all three are necessary, and in practice the terms on which the product is divided between those who supply the various types of labour, capital and natural resources depends largely on their relative bargaining power, which reflects the forces of supply and demand in the market. In this sense, for instance, it is possible to argue that unorganized industrial workers, especially if labour is plentiful relative to capital, as it was in Britain during the last century, and particularly in the case of the less skilled labour, are in a weak bargaining position relative to the owners of capital, and that the return which the market gives them is an unfair one. In this sense, then, one can talk of exploitation, and the growth of trade unions was largely designed to counteract such a situation by organizing the workers so as to increase their bargaining power. On the other hand, at a time of full employment, such as the present, organized labour is in a very strong bargaining position.

There is also the important consideration that, typically, the labourer is dependent on his wages for his livelihood, whereas the capitalist is often a comparatively wealthy man with other sources of income. This is true, broadly speaking, for although there are many cases of large salaries being received from the sale of labour which has a particularly scarcity-value, such as that of film stars and Q.C.s, and also of small capitalists such as elderly ladies dependent on a meagre income from dividends, yet as we have seen, the unequal ownership of capital is a much greater source of inequality of incomes than the unequal earnings of labour. But the fault lies here primarily in the unequal ownership of capital, and this is largely the result of inheritance. Inheritance also is the reason for the fact that the income from capital ownership so often does not reflect the fruits of saving actually undertaken by the person who receives it. We must be careful, therefore, not to confuse the question of payment for the use of capital with that of the distribution of the owner-ship of capital.

There remains the question whether it is 'right' that the act of saving and making savings available should carry with it an entitlement to draw an income in return. In economic theory, interest and dividends have been held to include a number of different elements. First of all, there is the reward for 'absti-nence' or 'waiting'—i.e. abstaining from present consumption and waiting for a greater return later, and thus setting resources free to be used as capital. Along with it goes the reward for 'sacrificing liquidity', that is for making one's savings available for investment instead of merely hoarding them in the bank or in an old stocking, so as to keep them 'liquid' for future use. Then, when we consider the actual return from any particular investment, there are two other elements. First there is a risk premium; a risky investment will normally have to pay a higher rate of interest, if it is to secure capital, than one like a govern-ment stock, on which the risk is very slight. Finally, and especially in the case of ordinary shares in joint-stock companies, there is the element of 'pure profit', with the corresponding risk of loss, which is the return for taking the risks of enterprise, and falls on the nominal owners of a business concern.

Can these various functions be regarded as essential services to production, in the same way as the supply of labour, in all its grades from unskilled labourer to general manager, and there-fore as equally entitled to a share in the product? A moral comparison of their respective value cannot easily be under-taken and is likely to be largely subjective. Certainly to talk, for instance, of 'abstinence' as a moral virtue on the part of a millionaire who saves because he cannot spend all his income seems absurd. We can, however, be certain that all these functions are economically essential; they must be performed

by some means or other in any form of organization of the productive process, especially one which makes use of modern
capitalistic methods. The diversion of resources from consumption or liquidity to be used as capital, the allocation of capital
between undertakings of varying degrees of risk, and the undertaking of the risks of enterprise are functions which must be
carried out somehow, and there must be some incentive to
encourage their performance and some mechanism to regulate
it. In the free enterprise system they are carried out by means
of the inducement of varying rates of interest and dividends,
and these interest rates also act as a price mechanism, allocating
the supply of capital between competing uses. Owing to the
importance of the self-regarding motive in human calculations,
it is unlikely that capital would be spontaneously made available
without such inducement. There must be some incentive to
secure the forgoing of consumption and the undertaking of the
necessary savings, and, if it is not done, as under free enterprise,
through the inducement of a share in the proceeds of investment,
then it must be done, as under planning, by deliberate decision
of the central authorities. This remains broadly the choice
available, even though nowadays an increasing part of our saving
is done corporately, through the ploughing back of undistributed profits by companies, and through the surpluses of public
authorities. But even if the rate of interest is abandoned as an
incentive to saving, it is apt to remain necessary as a regulator
of investment. Even in planned economies, it is found desirable
to use a nominal rate of interest to allocate the supply of capital
between alternative uses, and to require state undertakings to
meet this charge as an incentive to efficiency.

The payment of interest is thus to be regarded primarily as
a practical necessity to secure a supply of savings and to ensure
its allocation between competing uses. It is an imperfect device,
and its use may open the way to injustices, especially in the
form of inequality of incomes. Steps may have to be taken to
counter these injustices, as we have seen, but we cannot abandon

interest payments and the profit motive without giving up free enterprise altogether, and replacing it by some form of total planning, with all the difficulties which that brings in its train. To say this is not to refuse to recognize that there are 'contradictions in capitalism'. Some of them are of a serious nature, and we have already discussed them earlier. It is, however, to recognize that they have their essential origin at a deeper level than the outward form of economic organization; they go right down into the depths of the human heart. While steps can be taken to mitigate their consequences, they cannot be eliminated altogether by any alterations of the economic system, however radical.[1]

B. The Just Price.

The doctrine of the Just Price was another essential part of medieval Christian thinking about economic matters. Its prevalence was a testimony to the belief that the principles of Christian morality ought to apply in all areas of life, and that Christian ethics were just as much concerned with business as with theology or personal relations. The essence of the doctrine was that buyers ought to pay, and sellers receive, a price which was fair and just for the goods or services supplied, a price which covered the seller's costs plus a fair return for his own services. A corollary of this belief was that it was immoral for traders to take advantage of the exigencies of the market, by buying cheap in times of plenty, and selling dear in times of scarcity. Such practices were heartily condemned and efforts made to suppress them.

With the breakdown of the medieval idea of the unity of all

[1] A word needs to be said here about the problem of Stock Exchange speculation, which causes disquiet to many people. If capital is to be raised by the issue of stocks and shares, it is essential that there should be a market in which these can be freely bought and sold, so that those who wish to realize their holdings, or acquire new ones, can do so. Otherwise people would be unwilling to take the risk of tying up their capital in this way. Unfortunately, this opens the door to speculation in securities of a type which is little more than gambling. The problem is to find some means of checking such abuses without hampering the legitimate functions of the Exchange.

knowledge and the rise in modern times of the idea that economic affairs form a separate department of life, with its own independent rules, this ideal has disappeared from economic thought. The price mechanism is thought of as a device for equating supply and demand and allocating supply between competing uses. Thus it comes to be thought to be right and natural that traders should buy as cheaply as they can and sell as dearly; in doing so, they are performing their economic function of transferring goods from areas and times of relative plenty to those of scarcity. Reliance is placed upon competition in the ranks both of buyers and sellers to prevent price fluctuations from becoming excessive, for a rise of prices will induce an influx of supply and choke off some of the demand, while a fall of prices will choke off an excess supply and stimulate increased demand, and mobility of buyers and sellers will tend to keep prices fairly uniform throughout a given market.

We have already seen that a free market system, in which the price mechanism performs the allocation in this way, has great advantages in the way of flexibility and automatic working over any alternative system, such as allocation by rationing and administrative controls. Yet the ideal of the Just Price, although it finds little place in economic theory, still persists in its appeal to the imagination. It still has its practical applications in the field of policy. Some are mainly beneficial, as when stabilization schemes are introduced for agricultural products to prevent the hardships to producers and consumers alike which result from the violent price fluctuations characteristic of goods in highly inelastic supply in the short period. Others, such as price maintenance schemes devised by trade associations, are less beneficial, since they tend to provide stability for the trader at the expense of the customer and to eliminate the force of price competition as a stimulus to efficiency.

Thus the influence of the ideal of the Just Price remains as witness to the belief that ethical considerations ought to prevail over purely economic ones. Although the price mechanism may be fulfilling its economic function when sellers sell as dearly as they can and buyers buy as cheaply as they can, yet we feel that ethical duty demands that such attitudes should not be pressed to the full. We feel that the action of the grasping buyer or seller, determined to exact the utmost of advantage, is anti-social, and that commercial relationships should be tempered with charity. There should be that degree of give and take which recognizes and respects the interests of the other party. And this is a sound instinct, for inequalities of economic power are too great for reliance to be safely placed on the pursuit of self-interest as an infallible means to efficiency. Such charity in commercial dealings is only another recognition of the limitations of self-interest.

And it is in this sense of a tempering influence that the concept is most valuable. For when we come to try to define what a just price is, in any particular case, we do not get very far. We can only say that it is a price that is fair both to buyer and seller, and to arrive at this we cannot do more than take a 'fair market price', one which does not make the buyer pay more than he would have to pay under existing conditions of supply and demand, nor deprive the seller of the return which he could fairly get under such conditions. In other words, it is not possible to lay down *a priori* conditions for determining a just price, without regard to prevailing market circumstances.

c. An agricultural versus an industrial economy.

The other two problems are of more recent development and are bound up with the rise of modern industrialism. In recent years much attention has been focused on the unsatisfactory social aspects of present-day industrial society. The predominance of acquisitive motives in the economic organization of society, the lack of opportunity for satisfaction of the sense of vocation and creativity in the daily work of so many, the unsatisfactory physical environment provided by the drabness and the slums of modern industrial cities, the need to compensate monotonous work with exciting and often artificial pleasures, even the breakdown of Christian moral standards and the rise of juvenile crime in recent years; all these evils are real and disturbing enough. There has been a tendency, therefore, to seek an explanation of them in the artificiality of an industrial society, as compared with the healthier and more natural social order of a less complex agricultural and craft society. In the case of Britain in particular, these arguments have been reinforced by consideration of the precariousness of an economy largely dependent on the import of its staple foodstuffs and raw materials, and on the sale of manufactured goods to the rest of the world, at a time when industrialization is increasing in the agricultural countries and world population is likely to outpace food supply.

There is no doubt that there is much that is unhealthy in modern society, and that the root of it is largely a false sense of values, a valuing of material riches as an end in themselves instead of merely as a means which, if properly used, may make easier the approach to the worth-while life. The possibility of a more abundant supply of goods and services, including luxuries and conveniences formerly undreamed of, which industrialization has brought about, has naturally led to an undue emphasis on their desirability. When one's neighbours have smart clothes and furniture and television sets, one naturally comes to want them for oneself, especially when their desirability is constantly being emphasized by films and advertisements. But in the more sweeping condemnations of modern society which are common to-day, there is a certain confusion of thought and a certain unwillingness to face historical facts.

In the first place, the tendency is to compare modern society as we know it with an idealized version of the past, and thus to minimize both the gains of industrialism and the defects of the old order. It is true that in the agricultural and craft societies of the past there was a closer and more direct dependence on the processes of nature and hence probably a greater awareness, even if unconscious, of the natural values which underlie a healthy society. There was less scope for the worship of material wealth, because there was less scope for its production. Possibly also there was more scope for a sense of creativeness in daily work for many people at a time when the bulk of the population were closely connected with work on the land and many of the others were craftsmen exercising traditional skills. But the picture was not so ideal as we are sometimes tempted to think. There was a great deal of sheer arduous, monotonous drudgery, which had to be performed by human muscles because there were no machines to do it. Probably the numbers who had the opportunity of exercising the creative skill of craftsmen were always comparatively small, compared with those who experienced only the drudgery. Except in a few more favoured times and places, such as the seventeenth and eighteenth centuries in Britain, where trade and industry were already rapidly developing, an adequate supply of food and clothing and shelter was always a doubtful quantity for the bulk of the people. Modern medical and sanitary knowledge were lacking, and dirt and disease took a heavy toll. It is true that work was not performed under the vast and often impersonal organization of many modern factories, but there was plenty of scope for greed and brutality and bad working conditions on the farm and in the workshop.

Nor should we minimize the achievements of industrialism because we are conscious of its defects. The gain in the reduction of drudgery through the use of machines has been enormous. So also has been the gain in the standard of food, clothing, housing and amenities and comforts enjoyed by the ordinary man and woman in the industrialized societies of the west. Increased productivity has provided the wealth to make possible widespread provisions for medical and health services and for education. It has also provided a margin of leisure over and above working time for the enjoyment of a wider range of interests.

We must not forget, of course, that these gains have been confined to certain parts of the world only, nor the fact that they have been achieved to some extent by the exploitation of the resources of the rest of the world. Nor must we overlook the limitations which arise from the pressure of an increasing world population on a supply of natural resources which cannot be expanded so easily. But, as we saw earlier, the only hope of alleviating the poverty and suffering which are to be found still in so much of the world lies along the path of further industrialization.

Nor must we forget that a 'higher standard of living' in the material sense is no guarantee of increased satisfaction nor of an increase in true welfare. Still less is it necessarily a means towards the realization of the Kingdom of God. Yet we cannot but feel that it is God's Will that His children should enjoy these gifts, which have been made possible by the exercise of knowledge and skills which He has inspired, working on natural resources which He has given. And if it is true that a rise in material standards may be a stumbling block rather than a help in realizing the need for the true wealth which comes from God, that is a challenge which we have to face and accept. God has enabled us to develop machines and to build up mechanized industry and world-wide commerce. He has enabled us to reap many good gifts from them, but, because of our selfishness and fallibility, we have reaped many evil ones too, up to the point at which we are in danger of destroying the very civilization which we have created, through the use of atomic power in warfare. But that does not mean that industrialism and the use of machines are wrong, only that through human folly they have been wrongly used.

As for us here in Britain, we have little choice in the matter. Although it is probable that cheap imported foodstuffs may never be as plentiful again as they were in the earlier part of the present century so that we may have to grow more of our own food, yet the fact remains that there are fifty millions of us in this island, with very limited natural resources. Our greatest asset is our industrial and commercial skill and experience, and we shall have to rely mainly on them for our living. Self-sufficiency, even if it were desirable, is not practical for us.

Our conclusion must be, therefore, not that an industrial society is somehow 'wrong' and 'unnatural', whereas an agricultural one is 'natural', but rather that, along with the undoubted benefits of our industrial society, there are many serious defects. If these are to be remedied, it will be by a fuller understanding of the purposes of God in the economic and social order, so that we can see more clearly how He would have us use the powers which He has given us. We must accept industrialism, with all the potentialities of which it is capable, and seek to use it to God's glory, rather than trying to go back to a past which cannot be recovered. It may well be true that, in exploiting the productive powers of modern industry, we have tended towards an undue exaltation of material wealth, and that a healthier social order might be one in which the material standard of living was somewhat lower. In particular the highly industrialized nations of the west may be called upon to make some sacrifice in order to help the less developed parts of the world. It may also be true that certain aspects of the organization of modern industry tend to do violence to the personality of those who have to work under them, and that modifications will be required even at the expense of some material sacrifice. Nevertheless it remains true that industrialism must be accepted as an instrument of God's purposes rather than rejected. For, if one thing is certain in history, it is that you cannot put the clock back.

D. The monetary system.

Another tendency in recent years, which has its roots in the traditional ideas about usury, is to seek an explanation for the evils of the modern world in an unsound monetary system. The unsoundness is felt to lie in the existence of a 'money market', in which individuals and firms make profits by dealing in the various forms of credit, such as bank loans, bills of exchange and short-term securities. It is suggested that to do this involves the danger of making money into an end in itself, a commodity which can be bought and sold for its own sake, instead of merely a means to facilitate the transfer of resources and the stimulation of economic activity. The whole effect is accentuated by the atmosphere of mystery that is felt to surround the operations of high finance. Because the working of the monetary and banking system is difficult to understand, it is easy to suspect that there is some sort of sinister 'money power' which perverts the working of the economy for its own benefit.

Once again, it must be pointed out that a certain amount of confusion of thought and a good deal of over-simplification lies behind such a view. The monetary and financial system has grown up to meet the needs of industry and commerce, to provide the means of payment and of credit essential to the functioning of the modern world-wide economy. On the whole, it is not true that money and credit instruments have come to be thought of as ends in themselves, even by those who make their living by dealing in them. Money is not valued as an end in itself, but rather as a means to an end. What is bought and sold in the money market is the means of payment and of holding wealth, command over resources which can either be spent now on consumption or on investment, or held liquid to be spent later. Industrialists need credit to finance the purchase of raw materials and the payment of wages and other expenses until their product is ready for sale, traders need credit to buy and hold stocks, governments need credit to finance expenditure in anticipation or in excess of tax revenue. Persons or institutions with liquid funds need some form of short-term investment, such as Treasury Bills or bank deposit accounts, in which to hold them until they are needed for spending, or until an opportunity arises for profitable investment. In addition to supplying credit, the banking system provides a convenient means of transferring funds and accounting for transactions without the need for the actual handling of large quantities of coins and notes.

Money and the financial system exist primarily to perform essential services such as these, and bankers and bill-brokers and others engaged make their living primarily by supplying such services. Like the rest of our economic system, the money market works under the stimulus and the regulation of the profit motive. Therefore, like the rest of the system, it is liable to the dangers which arise from the abuse of this motive. Undoubtedly there is speculation in monetary instruments, and undoubtedly some of this speculation has harmful rather than valuable results, just as some forms of speculation in commodities can do. One example of these dangers is to be seen in the feverish and often quite unreal booms in Stock Exchange prices, followed by disastrous crashes, which were so common in Britain in the last century, and of which the Wall Street boom of 1929 was another striking case. Another example is to be seen in the panic movements of short-term funds from one country to another in search of security, which were such a menace to the stability of the exchanges around the time of the depression of 1929-32. It is often necessary to take steps of the 'planning' type, either by direct government action or otherwise, to deal with dangers of this sort. For instance, most governments have found it necessary in recent years to impose controls on the movement of capital funds into and out of the country, and also, in conditions of threatened inflation, to attempt to restrict the granting of credit facilities for the financing of Stock Exchange speculation.

The root of our economic problems lies deeper than the outward form of the monetary system or any other part of the machinery. There may be a case for certain changes in our monetary organization; we are not concerned to argue this at the moment; but there is no case for denouncing the monetary system in particular as 'unsound'. The unsoundness arises rather from a false sense of values which permeates the whole economic order. It is significant that recent economic theory is inclined to the view that purely monetary factors play a relatively small part in economic disorders, compared to the real factors which underlie them. Unsound credit policy may accentuate the fluctuations of the trade cycle and the resultant evils of unemployment or inflation, but it does not cause them. Similarly, sound monetary policy, in the narrow sense, is not enough by itself to cure them. 'Cheap money', in the sense of easier credit facilities, has only a very limited effect in stimulating economic activity at a time of deep depression; it needs to be accompanied by more vigorous measures such as large-scale government spending. Similarly, a restriction of credit facilities will not do enough by itself to counteract inflation, unless accompanied by measures such as increased taxation and reduced government spending. Nor is it much good seeking a solution for international economic disequilibria merely by devising a new method of regulating the exchanges, without also taking steps to deal with the real causes of persistent debit or credit balance of payments. The inefficacy of the International Monetary Fund[1] in the face of a world-wide dollar shortage made this abundantly clear in the first few post-war years, and so did the failure of the restored Gold Standard in the 1920's, in the face of the unresolved disequilibria which resulted from the first world war.

The monetary bogy is thus largely a false one, a confusion of one of the symptoms of disorder, or one of many contributory causes, with the underlying root cause. Monetary panaceas, like all forms of panacea, are therefore based on an over-simplification of the issues involved.

[1] The International Monetary Fund was established in 1945 and embodied the principles laid down by the Bretton Woods Conference of 1944. It was intended to facilitate the establishment of a system of multilateral exchanges. This it does by providing its members with the means to meet temporary small-scale adverse balances in their current payments. Unfortunately, its machinery has not proved adequate to meet dollar shortages on the post-war scale.

3. *Christian Action in the Situation.*

In what ways, then, can the responsibility of Christian witness be carried out in an economic order such as we have been considering? We have seen that economic activity is an essential part of the total of human life, but that just because of this it cannot be separated from the other aspects of life. Our economic witness is part and parcel of the witness of our whole lives, and each reacts on the other, so that our Christian witness as a whole is ineffective if we are not trying to take our economic responsibilities seriously. We have also seen that there are no easy short cuts. We cannot devote our energies entirely to advocating some particular 'Christian' form of economic organization, nor can we concentrate on one single aspect of the economic system, such as money or industrialization, in the hope that, if this is put right, the whole will then work satisfactorily. Moreover, our responsibility is both an individual and a collective one. We each have our own particular part to play in the economic system, as consumers, producers and citizens, but we are also members of the Church, which has corporate witness to make. We shall treat the individual responsibility first.

A. The witness of Christian individuals and groups.

The chief lines of responsibility for Christian witness by individuals and groups can be summarized for convenience under six main heads. These do not, of course, represent water-tight compartments, and the types of activities described under them will in practice often overlap.

(i) *Stewardship.*

The first responsibility is that of stewardship, the right use in God's service of income, talents, time and opportunities. Through the way in which we spend our incomes, the goods and services which we buy, the extent to which we save, and what we do with our savings, we exercise an influence on the working of the economic system, and, although the influence of the individual may be small, yet it should be responsibly exercised. This has an obvious importance, for instance in times of inflationary pressure, when the need is for less consumption and more saving, but the pull of institutional influences and natural inclinations is all the other way. It is true that consumption is the end-purpose of production, that the purpose of the economic system is ultimately to provide goods and services for the use and enjoyment of men. In this sense, there should rightly be a sort of spontaneity about our spending of our incomes. We should accept and use God's gifts thankfully, not indeed squandering them recklessly, nor grabbing them selfishly without consideration for others, but spending them ungrudgingly and without our enjoyment being marred by over-great carefulness. At the same time, we must be responsible and charitable in our use of them, both directly through our consideration of the needs of those with whom we come into immediate contact, and indirectly, through consideration of the effects of our stewardship on the way in which the needs of our fellowmen can be met through the proper working of the system.

We are also called to the exercise of stewardship of our gifts and talents, our time and our energies, and this leads us on to the second main line of witness, that of vocation.

(ii) *Vocation*.

Most of us have to earn our own livings, and even if we do not have to, as Christians we should want to do some work for the service of the community. Hence it is through our daily work that we make our most direct impact on the functioning of the economy as a whole.

The Christian doctrine of work is usually summed up by saying that the Christian must see his work as a vocation or calling. What do we mean by this? First of all, a recognition that work is an essential part of God's purpose for us, something to which He calls us. It is our contribution of skill and effort to the common task of sharing in God's creative designs, and the means by which, in return for our contribution, we share in the fruits of the common labour. Therefore, there is no shame in admitting that we work for a living, for that is what we are called to do, but in doing it we shall try to see our contribution as a service to God and our fellow-men. We shall try to give of our best, not thinking primarily of the direct return which we shall get in the form of income, but of the offering which we can make. We shall, of course, fail in this, and shall find ourselves being influenced by selfish desires to achieve gain or avoid discomfort, but the quality of our work will be affected nevertheless by the fundamental attitude towards it which we adopt. This is not to suggest of course that the aim of getting our living through our work is a wrong one or that it should be absent from our thoughts. It is part of the purpose of work that we should earn a living through it for ourselves and our dependants, and this motive cannot be absent from our attitude to it. But if we are trying to serve God, in response to His love for us in Christ, who earned his living as a carpenter, then we shall try to make the primary motive that of service to Him.

If, then, we are trying to think of our work as a service and to give of our best in it, it follows that we must do it with all our understanding. We must try to appreciate more fully the part which our own particular job plays in God's purposes, the contribution which it makes to the welfare of our fellows, so that we can do it in the best way in which we can. This will, of course, affect our choice of work, in so far as we have the opportunity to choose. Obviously, there are some jobs which it is much easier to see as a service to God and man than others, particularly those in which there is a direct personal contact with those to whom services are rendered, or those in which there is the satisfaction of taking a creative part in making some article which will be of direct use to another. Thus it is easier for the teacher in his class, or the shop assistant serving the housewife with her daily necessities, or the farm worker tending his crops, or the shoemaker making shoes, to realize his sense of vocation, than it is for the factory worker on the mass-production job or the clerk in the office. There are some jobs which appear to be concerned with producing goods or services of little apparent value, except that people want them and are willing to pay for them, such as some types of trivial luxury goods or personal services. There are other jobs which, although they may be essential, are in themselves so monotonous and uninteresting that it is difficult to see them as a vocation. A lot of the repetition work in modern industry is of this sort, and so is much routine clerical work. To those engaged on such tasks, the ultimate use of their services must often appear so remote, and their own share in it so small, that it is difficult for their imaginations to be inspired by any sense of social purpose in it. Then there are other jobs which are concerned with providing goods and services which, though people are willing to pay for them, we may feel to be actually socially harmful, such as the drug traffic, or possibly certain forms of organized gambling or certain aspects of the supply of alcoholic refreshment. In fact, there may be some jobs in which we feel that we can have no part, because we cannot see them as part of God's purposes. Apart from these, however, it is possible to find a true vocation in any form of work which does help to meet men's genuine needs and to help them to enjoy God's good gifts, even if the part which we have to play in it may seem small and the work itself uninspiring.

The idea of vocation usually carries with it in our minds that of choice. We think of people having a vocation to the mission field, or to the ministry, or professions such as medicine or nursing or teaching, in the sense that they feel so strongly called to that particular type of service that they deliberately choose to follow it, it may be at some considerable sacrifice of income or comfort. In so far as we are free to choose our jobs, vocation does of course imply choice. It is our responsibility to choose as our life's work that line of service for which we are best suited by ability and temperament, and in which we feel that we can give of our best. But for most people the choice is usually very limited. The boy or girl leaving school often has only a very narrow range of factory or office jobs available to choose from. He, or she, may not feel very strongly about any of them and may make several wrong choices. Probably, after a few years, a young man finds himself settled down in a job which suits him fairly well and at which he is reasonably competent, but which does not wildly excite his imagination as a form of service. By this time he has responsibilities and he is too old to change, even if there is anything else to which he feels strongly attracted. Is it possible to have a sense of vocation in such circumstances? We must recognize that there can be a vocation of acceptance as well as of choice. We may be called to accept a particular job because that is the one we are doing, and which we cannot get out of doing, and to see in it the field in which we are to give our service to God. The dull, routine job seen like this will seem much more worth while than if it is done grudgingly and resentfully. Besides, even if we are lucky enough to be doing the job which we really want to do, there are times when even the most interesting work seems dull and routine, and all jobs have their element of drudgery as well as that of interest. All of us, therefore, have a share in the vocation of acceptance as well as in that of choice.

This responsibility of finding a vocation in our work is one of the most important pieces of witness which we can make, and one which involves a contribution which no one else but we can give. There is an urgent need of the contribution which laymen can make, who are trying to see their jobs, and the decisions and choices which they involve, in the light of what they believe to be God's purposes for his world. Although we all do lip-service to the concept of work as vocation, we are all of us apt to overlook our responsibilities in this matter, and to fall too easily into acceptance of the world's standards and values. The nature of work, under the conditions of modern industry and commerce, and how God is to be glorified in it, is something about which a great deal more thought is needed, and each of us can have our part in it.

(iii) *Fellowship—love in action.*

As well as to service, the Christian is called in his economic activities to fellowship. We saw earlier that work is intended to be a means of fellowship, a form of loving co-operation between neighbours, and the same applies to all forms of economic relationship. We are called to work out the meaning of love in action, in our relationships with our colleagues and work-mates, in our business contacts with clients and customers, or with shopkeepers, bus conductors and all others with whom we come into touch.

Some of these contacts are deep and lasting and offer scope for a real self-giving on the part of all concerned. In this con-nection the work-group is probably the most important, for the people we work with are among those we get to know best and who get to know us best. For many men and women the chief satisfaction in work is to be found in fellowship with a friendly group of people, all engaged on the common task. This is often true, for instance, of groups of workers doing jobs which in themselves offer little interest or satisfaction. It is probably borne out by the experience of all of us. Whether the job itself is interesting or not, the work-group can offer its members a rich and satisfying experience of community. We can all of us give something towards making this fellowship fuller and more real, for we know that this is God's purpose. Those of us who are in positions of influence or authority have an especial responsi-bility here, for our attitude can vitally affect the well-being of our fellows.

Other economic contacts, such as those between client and

worker in the shop or bus or office, are necessarily briefer and more formal. Yet even here the attitude we adopt towards our fellows can make a great difference, and this is really the root of the matter. Do we treat those with whom we have contacts, at work or in business, as things or as persons? Are we trying to use them as a means to our own satisfaction, whether it be to get what we want out of them or to make them do what we think best for them against their will? Or are we really thinking of them as persons, with wishes and feelings and rights of their own, to be treated with the consideration and respect due to brothers and sisters for whom Christ has died? The root of true fellowship is in this recognition of persons as persons, with whom a relationship of mutual respect and mutual give and take is required, who have claims on us in their own right and can offer us their friendship in response to our own. The relationship must be an 'I—thou' one, not an 'I—it' one.

It is often very difficult to make this sort of fellowship a reality especially if we are concerned with the running of a large organization, in which for planning and administration purposes men and women must be treated to some extent as units, simply because there are too many of them to treat each one of them individually. The managers of a large industrial concern cannot have a direct 'I—thou' relationship with each of the many thousands of their employees. But even though this sort of impersonal treatment of men and women is inevitable, yet the realization that fundamentally they are persons will make all the difference to the way in which it works out in practice. The managers will try to treat their own immediate staffs as persons, and will so treat any of their employees with whom they come into personal contact. Their subordinates, if so treated, will be more likely to do the same, and so on throughout the organization. And in their thinking and their planning of the work of the undertaking, it will make a difference if they remember that they are concerned with individual men and women and not merely with 'hands' or 'units of manpower' or 'man-hours', convenient and necessary as these forms of measurement may be.

(iv) *Citizenship—political responsibilities.*

We exercise our economic responsibilities not only as consumers and producers, but also as citizens. As citizens we have our share in responsibility for the ordering of those functions which are carried out collectively by the State on behalf of the community. With the increasing part taken nowadays by the State in the ordering of economic affairs, questions of economic policy are coming to play an increasingly important part in political programmes and controversies. The level and nature of taxation, the extent and direction of government spending on social services, the effects of rearmament, how to deal with a rising cost of living, whether there should be more, or less, controls, the extent of control over foreign trade and exchanges, nationalization and the organization of nationalized industries: all these are topical questions in Britain and in a large part of the world to-day. Therefore, if we are to play our part as citizens, we must be in a position to make an informed and responsible contribution to the formation of public opinion on such questions.

We may feel that we ourselves have little opportunity for effective influence on such matters. The problems involved are often complex, and experts disagree on them. The actual decisions are taken by the Government, and we only have the opportunity, once every few years, of choosing in very general terms between two alternative governments with two alternative proposed policies. But although we can only cast our vote infrequently, and although the choice we then have to make is in such general terms, yet parliamentary government depends for its healthy functioning on the existence of an enlightened and alert public opinion. It is public opinion which largely influences what the policies will be which the political parties will put forward at election time, and public opinion also greatly influences the decisions and choices which the Government makes on specific issues of policy during its period of office. It is true that for the detailed knowledge on which to make up our minds we must usually rely on the experts, but experts differ, and on the basis of their recommendations there is usually a choice between several alternative lines of practical policy. Public opinion is very influential in deciding which of these shall be chosen. We can all play our part in the formation of public opinion, for we all of us have some influence on those around us, and the sounder and more informed we show our judgment to be the greater is likely to be our influence. By taking the trouble to find out the facts and weigh up the judgments of others, as far as we have the opportunity, and by giving thought to the formation of our own opinions, we are therefore making a valuable contribution to a healthier and juster social order.

As Christians we shall, of course, seek to do this in the light of our understanding of God's purposes for man and society. The thinking of Christians should act as the salt to keep the discussion active and healthy. In particular, Christians, who seek to hold all their opinions and ideas under the judgment of God, can help to act as a corrective to the forces of self-interest. There is a great danger that particular classes or economic interests, especially if they are strongly organized, will come to mistake their own immediate interests for those of the community. The power of pressure-groups can often be very strong. Christians are not immune from this danger, but they should be better able to hold their own beliefs and interests under judgment, and to consider the problems of the day as they affect the interests of others. They should, therefore, be less likely to oppose measures valuable to the community as a whole because their own immediate interests are adversely affected by them, and less likely also to support measures which benefit or do not injure themselves, without consideration for their effects on the interests of others. Thus the Christian in the exercise of his responsibilities as citizen can contribute a valuable detachment from self and a readiness to appreciate the opinions and interests of others.

(v) *Thought.*

In considering the part which Christians can play in the formation of public opinion, we have been led on to consider the responsibility of thought. It is on the Christian layman, engaged in his daily work, that the main responsibility rests of thinking out what is the significance of the Faith for the economic order. The clergyman, with his specialized theological and pastoral training, and his specialized work to do, has not the time or the experience of the actual job of getting a living in the workaday world to fit him to undertake it himself. Though he can give essential guidance on the basic meaning of the Faith, it is only the man who is working at a particular job who can work out how God is to be served and glorified in the factory, or office, or shop, or whatever it may be.

Here, of course, it must be stressed that there are differences of responsibility, according to talents and opportunities. Obviously, some people are fitted, by temperament and brain, interest, education, environment and the nature of their job, for one type of work, such as the study of the theological implications of economics, while others may be led more towards thinking out in a group with their fellows some of the practical problems involved in their day-to-day work, and others find their vocation amply fulfilled in the faithful carrying out of their own daily duties. The academic economist does not have the same interests or opportunities as the business executive, and his in turn are different from those of the trade union official, or civil servant, or doctor, or lawyer, or shopkeeper, or the man or woman at the bench. But each of us has some contribution to make, some fruit of our own experience and our own thinking, under God's guidance, and if His Will is to be done it is up to us to make it.

In particular, the pooling of the experience of men and women of different backgrounds and different ways of thinking who share a common concern for some problem can often be extremely fruitful. There has been a good deal of experimentation recently with groups of this sort, notably the work done under the auspices of bodies such as the Christian Frontier Council,[1] but there is need for a good deal more, especially at a more local and informal level. Among the lines of approach which have been found to be fruitful are meetings of members of a particular profession or trade, to consider the problems which they come across in the course of their daily work. Another possibility is the meeting together of those who have to deal with similar problems from different points of view, such as managers, trade union officials and civil servants. Meeting together in groups is particularly valuable, in that the sharing of views and experiences stimulates the thinking of the individual members, and out of the interplay of opinions comes both a wider understanding and a clearer vision of the nature of the problems concerned. It can therefore be one of the most important and effective forms of Christian witness.

(vi) *Experiment.*

The responsibility of thought leads us on to that of experiment, and here the range of opportunity is even more varied. Most of us probably have little chance of carrying out experiments in order to see if the way in which we do our work can be brought more into accordance with the Will of God. Our opportunities are limited, and our responsibilities towards our families, our fellow-workers and those whom we serve by our work are too great for us to take many risks. But each of us has some initiative in the way we do our jobs or spend our incomes, and if we can see something which we can do that

[1] Two examples of the fruits of such groups, in book form, are Sir Walter Moberly's *The Crisis in the University* (London, 1949) and D. T. Jenkins's *The Doctor's Profession,* 1949). For a first-hand account of the work of the Christian Frontier Council and for a general discussion of these issues, see the quarterly periodical, *The Christian News Letter* (Oxley and Sons, Windsor).

M

seems to us worth trying in God's name, then we may feel it right to try it.

For some there will be greater opportunities, and there is a great need for the carrying out of experiments in economic organization, inspired by the desire to put into practice what are felt to be God's purposes. The lines of experiment which have been tried or suggested are many and various, but we can mention some of them briefly under three main heads.

(a) *Self-supporting communities* have been a common form of economic witness throughout the Christian era. In these, groups of men and women try to create a community in which work for mutual support and mutual enjoyment of the fruits will be deliberately organized as the corporate activity of a fellowship. In some cases, the aim is to be as fully self-sufficient as possible by growing their own food, making their own clothing and furniture and utensils and so on. In others, a greater part may be played by production for the market, using the proceeds to provide in common for the needs of the community. In either case, by their nature such communities are bound to be small-scale, with their emphasis, in these days when industry must usually be large-scale, mainly upon agriculture. They are bound by their nature also to involve a renunciation of material wealth in favour of a simpler style of living. As such they are a valuable form of witness to the wider economic order from which they are trying in a measure to separate themselves. They are an attempt to put into practice, in a small-scale model, the principles and the spirit which it is felt should underlie economic relationships. Thus there will always be a place for them, and in fact there are quite a number of them in existence to-day. Essentially, however, they can only be for the few.

(b) *Reorganization of existing patterns of enterprise—Co-operatives and Co-partnerships.* Many people have sought to reorganize existing enterprises, or to establish new undertakings so that, while engaged in production for the market in the usual way, they would reflect in their organization something nearer to the Christian ideal of brotherly co-operation. The aim was thus, not to contract out of the existing order as far as possible, as is the Community ideal, so much as to transform it from within.

One line along which this has been attempted has been through producers' co-operatives, in which the undertaking is owned jointly by those who work in it, who combine together to provide the necessary capital and share the risks, and divide the proceeds between them. A movement in this direction was strongly supported by F. D. Maurice[1] and the Christian Socialists of a century ago, and, of the producers' co-operatives started at this time under their inspiration together with that of idealistic Socialists of the Owenite[2] type, a few are still in existence to-day.[3] Such undertakings have usually been small, because of difficulties of organization, and have therefore suffered from the competition of larger joint-stock companies command- ing a much greater capital. They have also tended to come up against difficulties concerning the exercise of managerial authority over a group of workers all of whom are nominally equal partners. Consequently, little has been heard of them in recent years, except in more specialized forms, such as the farmers' co- operatives for the sale of produce and purchase of materials, which have been common in some countries.

Under this head, mention ought also to be made of the large and successful Consumers' Co-operative Movement, with its associated Wholesale Societies. This already plays a very large part in retail distribution and in certain types of manufacture,

[1] Frederick Denison Maurice (1805-1872) was a friend of Charles Kingsley and a leader of the Christian Socialists, who were led, by the inspiration of the Oxford Movement, to take a renewed interest in the social and economic order.

[2] Robert Owen (1771-1858), a successful and philanthropic mill-owner, became one of the first inspirers of the Socialist Movement. His socialism was of the 'Utopian' type denounced by Marx.

[3] Producers' Co-operative Societies federated in the Co-operative Productive Federation numbered 41 in 1939, with 14,514 members and 8,000 employees, and combined sales of rather under £3 million. G. D. H. Cole: *A Century of Co-operation* (London, 1946), p. 394

and more consideration might well be given by Christian thought to its implications. In this case the ownership of the retail societies is vested in the consumers, who become members of the society and receive dividends from the sales proceeds in proportion to their purchases. The retail societies in turn are members of the wholesale societies, which undertake manufacturing and wholesale trading activities on behalf of their constituents, and which pay dividends to the retail societies on their respective purchases. Control of the societies is constitutionally in the hands of their members, and, although the bulk of the members regard their societies merely as a particular type of store which pays a dividend, there is a good deal of social and educational activity carried on by the more active members. Although the scope of the Co-operative Movement in Britain has come to be largely limited to retail and wholesale trading and associated manufacture, yet it deserves consideration as a form of organization of economic activity alternative to the joint-stock company or the nationalized enterprise.[1]

The other line of approach was through what we can summarize under the term 'Co-partnership'. In this the starting point is usually an existing productive organization of the joint-stock company type, or else a new one to be established on a similar pattern, with a large investment of capital contributed by stockholders, and with a clear distinction between management and employees. The aim is usually to give certain defined rights and responsibilities to all those engaged in the concern, so as to inspire a sense of loyalty and obligation. Thus the employees may be given a share holding, guaranteed terms of employment and representation on the board of directors, while the shareholders' dividend and voting rights may also be limited and guaranteed. There has been a number of experiments which could be classified under this head. Some have involved little more than the distribution of shares carrying an entitle-

[1] For an account of the Co-operative Movement, see G. D. H. Cole: *A Century of Co-operation* (London, 1946).

ment to what is virtually a wage bonus, together with the encouragement of joint consultation. Others have involved the structural reconstruction of the undertakings concerned, in the light of definite and deliberately accepted principles of organization embodying the ideals of those responsible. So far, none of these experiments of the more far-reaching type has been large enough to modify to any extent the existing pattern of organization, but there is obviously scope for further experiment.[1]

(c) *Economic witness in income spending.* Experiments have not been lacking on the side also of the Christian witness of the consumer. Some Christians have felt the need of a more definite rule of spending, as an expression of their obligations of stewardship of God's gifts and of charity towards their neighbours. Renunciation in personal spending has of course been practised by innumerable Christians, but recently this desire has found expression in a number of organized movements. One of them is the 'National Average' movement, involving the resolution to spend on consumption, usually on a family basis, no more than the average income per family enjoyed in the country at the time in question. Another is the 'Economic Witness' recently developed under the auspices of the Iona Community[2] in which a group of people resolve to pool their surplus income over and above a certain minimum, depending on their commitments and calculated on the basis of income-tax allowances, the pool being spent according to the decisions of the group. Such experiments are inspired largely by a desire to make some sort of witness which will give effective expression to a Christian concern at the ill-effects of inequality of incomes. Obviously, the exercise of this responsibility of stewardship in

[1] For an account of one experiment of this kind, see *Partnership for All*, by J. Spedan Lewis (London, 1948).
[2] The Iona Community—a fellowship of ministers and laymen of the Church of Scotland, having as its centre of inspiration the island of Iona, and under the leadership of the Rev. Dr. George Macleod. For an account of the principles of 'Economic Witness', see the article by Dr. Macleod in the Community's magazine, *The Coracle*, No. 18, April, 1950.

consumption must be left to the decision of the individual, for each of us has his own commitments and interests, personal, family, charitable and so on. The existence of these movements, however, should act as a challenge to us to take our responsibilities seriously.

The mention of these various lines of experiment reminds us that we are called to active witness in the service of God, in the economic order as much as in the sphere of personal life. Although most of us must continue to get our living and do our jobs within the framework of the economic system as we know it, yet we must never rest content with it. We must always be alert for ways in which God's Will can be done more effectively. At the same time, we must not be tempted to try to 'contract out' of the economic system because we feel it to be imperfect, nor to feel that we can escape our share of responsibility for this imperfection. We are in the world, and involved in its evil, but we have also experienced its salvation. God has work for us to do in making this known in the circumstances of our own situation and our witness is just as valuable, even if it is quite unspectacular and appears to be unnoticed.

B. The Corporate Witness of the Church.

We Christians are not isolated individuals, we are members of the Body, the Church. In addition to our witness as individuals or in groups, there is the corporate witness of the Church to be considered. Since we are all members of the Church, this corporate witness is our witness, and we are all responsible for it. It is not something which can be left to the clergy, particularly, as we have seen, when the need is for the fruits of practical experience in the daily work of the world. Yet there is a sense in which the corporate witness of the whole Body is different both in method and in function from that of its members, and we need therefore to consider some of the lines which it should take.

The first and most essential witness of the Church is to be

itself. It is the community within which the redeemed life is shown forth, and hence the quality of its fellowship should witness to what God's purpose is for the true life of a community. Men should be able to see in the life of the Church that joyful and self-giving co-operation in which the life of the individual finds true fulfilment. It is thus essential that it should take care to free its own life of those false values which human fallibility always tends to allow to creep in. Distinctions of income, class, education, culture, race and nation should be seen to have no effect in marring the fellowship: rather, the common life should be enriched by the diversity of the offerings. There is thus a challenge to all of us, and plenty of scope for witness, for we all know that these distinctions do mar our fellowship at present.

It follows that the Church has a responsibility to see that the economic witness of its own life is helpful rather than harmful to the effectiveness of its life and mission. Great inequalities in the incomes of its clergy and other officers, and poverty among its clergy owing to unwillingness of the laity to accept their financial responsibility, are alike evils in this respect.

In addition to this primary responsibility to be itself, the Church has certain more specific responsibilities to the social and economic order which arise out of it. These we may briefly enumerate.

First of all, it must preach the Gospel. It must make known to men the goods news of God's love in Christ and what this redemption means in all aspects of life. It must proclaim God's purposes of justice and fellowship in a redeemed community and the need for repentance that His grace may be accepted.

Secondly, it has a teaching duty towards its own members, to help them to understand more fully the implications of the Faith for their own lives. In so far as this teaching must necessarily be theological, the responsibility for it must rest primarily on the clergy who are trained for it. In so far as the laity, by their practical experience or learning in other fields, can add something of value to it, they share in the responsibility. There is a great need in these days for what Sir Walter Moberly called 'lay theologians',[1] who can see the theological implications of their own particular branch of knowledge or sphere of activity.

Thirdly, it has a duty towards society to witness to the Will of God in actual situations and thus to hold the organization of society under judgment. When particular questions of policy arise, or particular social and economic problems must be dealt with, then the Church must witness to the moral principles and issues involved, and try to show forth the Will of God in this situation. This will not usually mean that the Church can or should take up an authoritarian position on the matter, dogmatically supporting one side or the other. Sometimes issues will rise which are so clear that this can be done. Examples which occur to one are those of the Abolition of Slavery, the introduction of the Factory Acts, and, more recently, the anti-Jewish campaigns of the Fascists, or the perversions of truth and justice practised by the Communists. More often the questions will involve a balancing of opposing advantages and disadvantages, and the making of choices on which Christians themselves, along with men of goodwill outside the Church, will sincerely disagree. The Church cannot pronounce dogmatically on the rightness or wrongness of the nationalization of basic industries, or of the Health Service, or of controls, or even on the question of participation in war. All these are matters which involve technical considerations on which Christians, as such, are no better qualified to give an expert opinion than others, and on all of them Christians of equal sincerity and qualifications will be found holding different opinions. What the Church can do, or rather what the leaders of Christian opinion can do in its name, is to make clear the issues of principle which underlie such questions, and in particular, the implications for them of Christian beliefs concerning the nature and purpose of man and society. Thus individuals will be enabled to make their own choices with a

[1] Cf. Sir Walter Moberly: *The Crisis in the University* (London, 1949).

clearer understanding, and with some idea of the likely consequences, both good and evil, of the different possible alternative
lines of action.

It is in ways such as these that the Church can fulfil its
responsibility for corporate witness to its own members and to
the world around. And it is from their membership of the
Church, from their sharing in its life and in the means of grace
entrusted to it, that its members will find the strength and the
guidance which they need for their own individual witness.

CHAPTER NINE

CONCLUSIONS

What conclusions can we draw from our study? We have been concerned to emphasize that the economic order is an essential part of the life of society, and that the life of society cannot be healthy unless the economic order is healthy. It is therefore essential that Christians should take seriously their economic witness, since it is part and parcel of the total witness of their lives. The economic order is intended to be the sphere in which men and woman co-operate to use, to God's glory and their own enjoyment, the riches which He has given them in the way of natural resources and human wisdom and skills. It has, however, been marred by sin. Man's self-expression, instead of being surrendered and sanctified in the service of his Creator, has been perverted to become a means of selfish greed and exploitation. In other words, both free enterprise and planning, as practised by unredeemed men, have their dangers and defects as well as their advantages. Since we must take men as they are, when considering the best ordering of society, it follows that in practice we need a blend of both. It is essential to preserve the positive elements of both, while using each to offset the dangers of the other. In the circumstances in which we find ourselves to-day, the best prospects probably lie along the lines of the planned framework, within which there is scope for free enterprise.

Christians, however, do not only claim to be able to see man as he is, with potentialities both for good and for evil. They also claim to have a gospel, good news of redemption for the whole universe, including the economic order. We have said a lot about the need to work out the meaning of redemption in economic terms, and we must try to draw out some conclusions about what this implies in practice. In the first place, it means that we try to get clear as to the real purpose both of our own particular work, and of the work of the society in which we are involved. How does our particular job fit into God's purposes for His world, both as regards the reasons for which we do it and the way in which we do it? How do the ways in which our community gets its living fit into these purposes, both as regards the aims and ideals which inspire them and the organizations and practice in which they find expression? At the same time we try both to adapt our own economic aims and actions accordingly, and to influence, as far as we have the opportunity, the economic aims and actions of our society. How does God want us to do our jobs so that we play our part more fully in the doing of His will? How should the ways in which our community gets its living be modified so that His will is more fully done? The Good News is that through the power of Christ this can be done, for by His love He overcomes our selfishness and blindness. In Him, therefore, we are enabled to see more clearly and our wills are strengthened to do what He would have done.

In Chapter VIII we were considering some of the ways in which these things might be done, and it is possible that at this stage the patient reader may have felt a measure of disappointment. After the analysis of the shortcomings of our economic order, when viewed in the light of God's purposes for it, where is the inspiring programme of action which we might have expected? What have we in the way of a dynamic to thrill the imagination and compete with the promises offered by the Communists? We are told that the best which we can hope for is something very like the Welfare State as we know it. We are told that the best we can do is to go on doing our daily jobs as well as we can and devote a bit more study and thought to the issues involved in them. The most fruitful line of action that is commended to us is to join a study group! Does it not all tend to boil down to saying that, although things are unsatisfactory, they might be a great deal worse, and that in any case, there isn't much more that we can do about it?

Such a criticism would be both true and false. There is certainly a danger of complacency, for once we realize that things are very complex, and that any changes which we may bring about are not short cuts to the millennium, we may be tempted to sit back and do nothing. This of course is wrong, for we have the responsibility of doing the best in the situation in which we find ourselves, even though the consequences may not turn out quite as we had hoped. It is, of course, true that ultimately the root causes of the defects of our economic system are moral and spiritual rather than organizational. Ultimately, the evil lies not in such things as the private ownership of the means of production, the growth of monopolies or the money market, but in the sinful hearts of men. Yet the picture is not as simple as that, for men's characters and motives, and their institutions and organizations, act and react on one another. Man's selfishness find expression in the evils associated with private ownership, monopolies, the money market and so on, and the forms of these institutions in turn influence the characters and motives of those involved in them. Though ultimately it is human selfishness which produces perverse institutions, yet at the same time perverse institutions can make men more perverse. Therefore it is important, and worth while, to be concerned with the forms of the economic order, as well as with its motives. We can help to bring about alterations in our institutions, so that they make it easier, instead of harder, for men to practise the sort of economic conduct that conduces to the glory of God and the spread of His kingdom.

Although it is fundamentally true that we want new men rather than new systems, it is not true that, if only we could get men changed it wouldn't matter about the outward forms.

For one thing, men are still fallible and limited in vision even when changed and cannot be relied upon to do what is right under God's guidance. Even when men are sincerely trying to do God's will, their judgments are still influenced by their cultural and institutional background, by the things which they take for granted as the basis of their thinking. We have grown up in a competitive, capitalist society, and our standards of judgment are influenced by the accepted values of such a society, even when we think that we are being most objective. Therefore we still have to use our brains and experience to think out what are God's purposes for the economic and social order. We need God's grace to help us to do it objectively and to enable us to devise the best form of organization to secure these purposes. We need to provide checks against our own selfishness and limited vision.

Nor will Christians agree which are the most important things to be done and which are the best ways to do them. Some will want more planning, for instance, and others more free enterprise. For another thing, Christians are a minority in the world and we cannot wait until everyone is converted. We have therefore the responsibility of seeing that God's Will is done in the outward ordering of society even at the same time as we seek to make His salvation known.

There is plenty for us to do, even though we cannot expect to find some particular programme of action or line of policy which we can put forward as the only, and infallible, ' Christian ' one. We cannot compete with the Communists, or anyone else, in the offering of panaceas, for we know that all forms of human organization are marred by sin. There are, however, many specific lines of action open to us which may remedy particular evils, even though they will bring other results, good and bad, in their train. We have to take our choice between them. We are especially called upon to do this in the field of our own daily work, for one of the greatest needs of the day is the discovery of the meaning of vocation as applied to work in a complex industrial society; and even though what lies before us may appear unspectacular, and its results limited and disappointing, we know that it is worth while, for we do it for Christ, and nothing truly done in His name is wasted. Christianity does offer a social dynamic, and it is sounder and deeper than that of the secular philosophies, but it makes demands both on our faith and our understanding.

BIBLIOGRAPHY

The following are some of the books which may be found useful for further reading:

INTRODUCTIONS TO ECONOMICS

Cairncross, A., *Introduction to Economics*, 2nd edition, London, 1951.

Clay, Sir H., *Economics for the General Reader*, 2nd edition, London, 1942.

Hicks, J. R., *The Social Framework*, 2nd edition, Oxford, 1952.

Phelps Brown, E. H., *A Course in Applied Economics*, London, 1951.

Pigou, A. C., *Income*, London, 1946.

Williams, G., *Economics of Everyday Life* (Penguin), London, 1951.

CHRISTIANITY AND THE SOCIAL AND ECONOMIC ORDER (GENERAL)

Barker, E., and Preston, R. H., *Christians in Society*, London, 1939.

Demant, V. A., *Religion and the Decline of Capitalism*, London, 1952.

Drucker, P. F., *The End of Economic Man*, London, 1939.
     The New Society, London, 1951.

Goyder, G., *The Future of Private Enterprise*, Oxford, 1951.

Schuster, Sir G., *Christianity and Human Relations in Industry*, London, 1951.

Tawney, R. H., *Equality*, London, 1931.
     Religion and the Rise of Capitalism, London, 1926.
     The Acquisitive Society, London, 1921.

Temple, W., *Christianity and the Social Order*, London, 1942.

191

Planning and Free Enterprise

Chester, D. N. (editor), *Lessons of the British War Economy*, Cambridge, 1951.

Devons, E., *Planning in Practice—Essays in Aircraft Planning in Wartime*, Cambridge, 1950.

Fisher, A. G. B., *Economic Progress and Social Security*, London, 1945.

Franks, Sir O., *Central Planning and Control in War and Peace*, London, 1947.

Jewkes, J., *Ordeal by Planning*, London, 1948.

Lewis, W. A., *The Principles of Economic Planning*, London, 1949.

Robbins, L., *The Economic Problem in War and Peace*, London, 1947.

Other Specific Topics

Beveridge, Lord, *Full Employment in a Free Society*, London, 1944.

Cole, G. D. H., *A Century of Co-operation*, London, 1946.

Dempsey, B. W., *Interest and Usury*, London, 1948.

Lewis, J. S., *Partnership for All*, London, 1948.

Morgan, E. V., *The Conquest of Unemployment*, London, 1947.

Roberts, M., *The Estate of Man*, London, 1951.
(A study of the exploitation of the world's material and human resources.)

Sayers, R. S., *Modern Banking*, 3rd edition, Oxford, 1951.

Withers, H., *The Meaning of Money*, 7th edition, London, 1947.